THE COFFEE
VISIONARY

THE COFFEE
VISIONARY

THE LIFE & LEGACY
OF ALFRED PEET

JASPER HOUTMAN

Roundtree Press
Petaluma, California

Table of Contents

"The coffee tells my story."

—Alfred Peet

No.

PEET, Alfred Henr

226 Divisadero St.

AR 10 1920 Date of orde

e issued   SEP

S. District   Court at   Sa

43791   Alien R

8182920

San Francisco, Cal

SEP 8 1960

admission

1960

by th

rancisco, California

INTRODUCTION

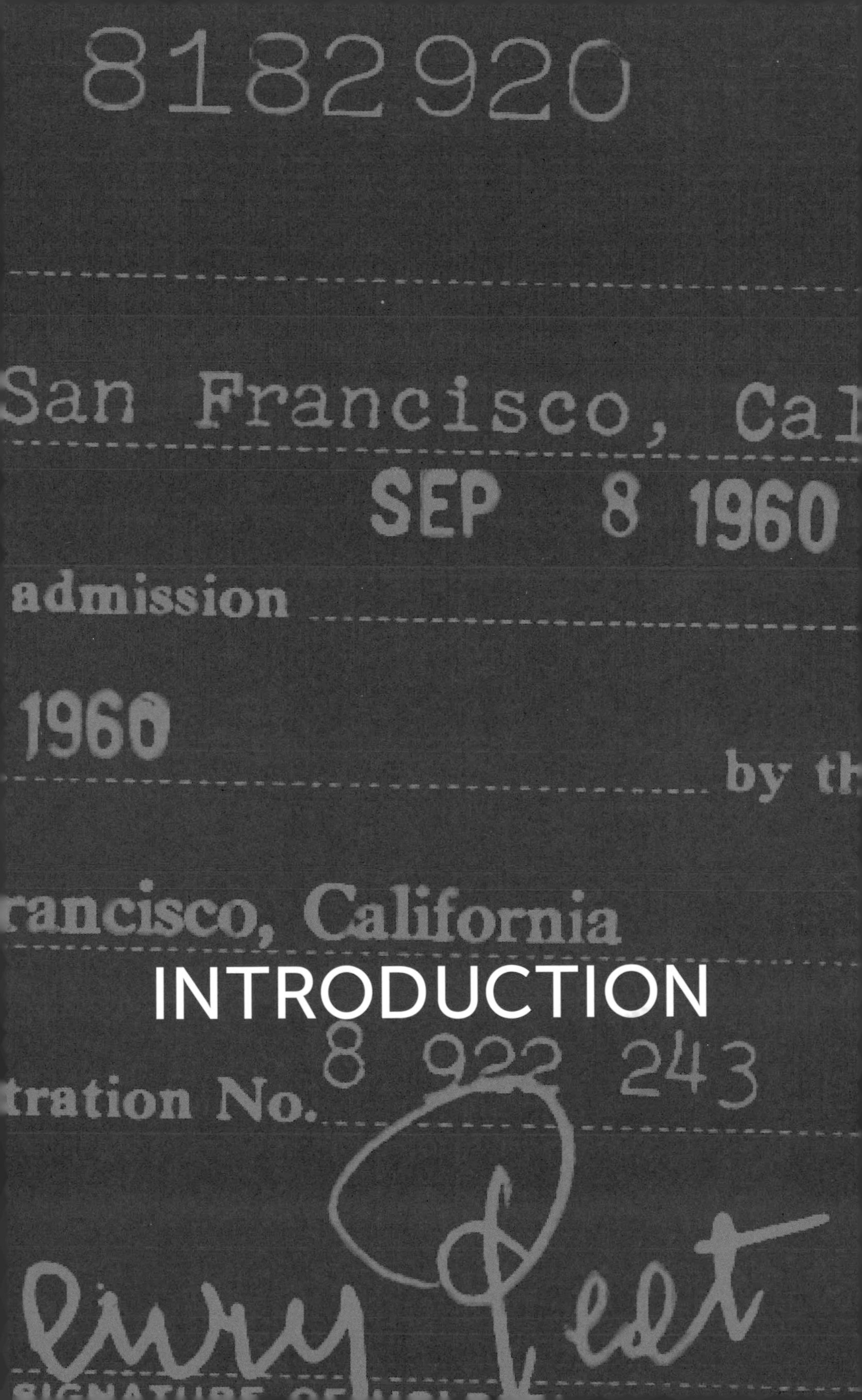

tration No. 8 922 243

ewry Peet

SIGNATURE OF HOLD

THE MAKING OF A COFFEE AFICIONADO

he man who, in 1966, started the iconic coffee chain Peet's Coffee was right about the coffee telling his story. If you want to know more about Alfred Peet and appreciate him, all you have to do is walk into any of the two hundred and fifty Peet's stores, buy a cup of coffee, and savor the delicious, dark brew.

And yet, you may wonder how the son of a coffee roaster from an average town in the Netherlands became the godfather of quality coffee in the United States. How had he managed to change an entire country's attitude toward coffee while operating from his small store in Berkeley? Who was Alfred Peet, the man who not only mentored the founders of Starbucks in the business of coffee, but also laid the foundation for "specialty coffee" and the coffee culture we see all around us these days?

I had been drawn in by the story of my fellow countryman for quite some time, perhaps more so because in the country of his birth Alfred Peet is hardly known, despite the huge impact he has had on the coffee world. I had already been mesmerized by coffee during a trip through Central America. It started with a question I was asked when I was served an espresso in Honduras: "How do you like the coffee?" It was the kind of question that could have come from Alfred Peet as he served coffee in his shop in Berkeley. He was uniquely gifted at pulling people in and making them pay attention to the coffee they were drinking, possibly even setting them on the path to becoming coffee aficionados.

To find out who Peet was and how he inspired so many to appreciate good coffee, I spoke to dozens of people who knew him, both in the United States and the Netherlands. Family, friends, and the people of Peet's tell their stories of Alfred Peet in this book. The founders of Starbucks show how important he was to them as a teacher and mentor. While I never spoke to Alfred Peet personally, he tells his own story in the (recorded) conversations he had with his friend, writer Adah Bakalinsky.

All the different puzzle pieces gave me a story that couldn't be told just by drinking coffee at one of his stores. It's a story of a man who traveled all over the world to find his final destination in the United States as a successful coffee entrepreneur with one guiding principle: Always aim for the best quality. He was a man who was known for his stubbornness, but he was also sensitive to the needs of others and could be very generous. Like all of us, he was constantly looking for his destiny in life and was lucky to find it in his love for coffee. By sharing his love for coffee, he made many people happy.

"It was a battle to educate customers."

—Alfred Peet

1

BERKELEY, 1966

H ow many entrepreneurs can say that they found success due to a dancing class? There is at least one who can make that claim. When Alfred Peet started his coffee business, there was one large doubt in his mind, but a dancing class solved all that.

"I've always known that I had it in me to become an entrepreneur," Alfred would say later, at the beginning of the eighties. "If my coffee business were to have failed, it wouldn't have been because of lack of motivation or talent or too little demand for better coffee. Failure could have to do with only one thing: the wrong location." The choice of location at the corner of Vine and Walnut Streets in Berkeley couldn't have been better. Alfred owed the discovery of the spot to Katherine Archer, whom he got to know at the beginning of the sixties when they took the same Scottish dancing class.

When I met Archer at Peet's on Vine Street in 2014, she characterized Alfred as "different." As we were talking, her eyes went around the interior of the store, and she said repeatedly that nothing had really changed. She had a picture of the early years of the store and showed me all the elements that were still the same, including the fifty-year-old bins where the coffee is kept.

Archer avoided Alfred during the dancing class at first, but she came to appreciate him. In a later interview, he'd describe her as a "very bright and intelligent woman." Soon after they got to know each other better, Alfred had disclosed to her that he wanted to start his own coffee business. "He wanted to introduce people to coffee that was roasted and prepared well. Then I told him about Berkeley, which could be a great place for a coffee business because of its proximity to UC Berkeley."

The building Archer took Alfred to had been empty for two years. It had been a paint shop that was forced to close because of a fire. It's not hard to imagine what the place must have looked like when they visited it for the first time. Archer advised Alfred, telling him that it was spacious enough for his plans and that people in Berkeley would be interested in the type of coffee store he had in mind. "It was true what she said. The building had everything I needed. In addition, the rent was reasonable because it had been empty for two years." Alfred would give Archer all the praise for finding the perfect spot for the first Peet's. "She pointed me to the location, so I can't take any credit for it."

Before he started his search for a suitable location in the Bay Area, Alfred had considered other US cities, such as New Orleans. But Louisiana weather was "too hot" for him. He had settled in San Francisco in 1955, and he considered cities to the north as locations for his store. But the reason those cities wouldn't do either may seem obvious: "Too cold." So the nice, mild climate of the Bay Area may have been one of the decisive factors in Alfred's decision to start his business in Berkeley.

NASCENT NEIGHBORHOOD

The neighborhood in Berkeley where Alfred opened his coffee store was relatively undeveloped. Not until the latter part of the nine-teenth century—when the University of California–Berkeley was founded—were more homes built in the area, but even then there was still enough land to have a cow near your house. The building of a train station triggered further development, according to Andrée

Abecassis, who writes about this in a book commemorating the twenty-fifth anniversary of Peet's.

Alfred's location consisted of a two-story building that was constructed of wood in a neoclassical architectural style. Built by a butcher named Louis Stein, who occupied the second floor with his family, the structure dated back to the beginning of the twentieth century. The ground floor was for business, becoming a restaurant, grocery, bakery, and paint store as the years passed.

Alfred didn't know Berkeley very well, and at first, he found the neighborhood much too quiet. "There was nothing. I remember a laundry which was run by a Chinese family, and there was an older woman who sold secondhand bags." However, the nearby university could potentially bring in people, he thought, just as Archer had suggested. The same applied to the supermarkets that had set up shop in this area of town (Lucky's, Safeway, and Co-op). "I thought, if I'm on a corner close to where such a tremendous number of people go to shop for groceries, if they like my coffee, they'll walk one block over to buy it. It was a good judgment, I must say."

Alfred hired a number of Chinese carpenters from nearby Oakland to build the counter, bins for the coffee, and other parts of the interior. "I designed it all myself—they made it the way I had envisioned it." Alfred himself installed the gas line for the coffee roaster he had purchased for the store. Until late in life, he was happy to take on such chores—though he wasn't always the kind of skilled handyman who should. Fortunately, the gas line was not a problem.

The coffee roaster Royal #5, purchased by Alfred, was already a classic. It was manufactured by the American company A.J. Deer, and besides coffee, it could also roast peanuts. Alfred roasted peanuts for a time, but stopped when it attracted mice; apparently, Alfred's cat did little to deter them.

In a well-known picture from those days, dating from the beginning of Peet's, you can see Alfred with the successor of the aforementioned roaster, which he bought when the capacity of the Royal #5 could not keep up with demand. In the picture, Alfred is leaning on the circular cooling bin, located near the roaster where the beans would fall to cool down. As always, he is dressed immaculately in a shirt, tie, and shopcoat. His gaze is penetrating, with eyes that are shielded by large black-framed glasses. The concentration one needs to roast can be perceived from his expression in the picture. But his posture also indicates: How can I help you?

The logo of the new store, which then still read Peet's Coffee, Tea & Spices, was marked by a sixties' style of design. It almost seems as if the designer grabbed it from the album covers of the Jimi Hendrix Experience and the Grateful Dead. Another designer, by the name of David Lance Goines, from Berkeley, designed the typography of the menu lists of Peet's. He also made a nice commercial poster for the store, but Alfred felt coffee wasn't prominent enough on the poster and asked the designer to destroy it, which he did. Later, it turned out that Alfred had actually kept a copy of the poster himself. The anecdote demonstrates that from the beginning, Alfred was deeply invested in every aspect of the branding of his store.

Thanks to the people who helped with the interior of the store, the place also obtained some remarkable lamps. In fact, the gold-colored lamps looked as though they were Middle Eastern, which wouldn't have been out of place for a local café. Archer remembered when the lamps were turned on for the first time, everyone was surprised by the red light they emitted. "Alfred said, 'Look at those lamps! If coffee fails, I can always turn it into a bordello.'" She had to laugh, thinking back on that moment and pointed up at the lamps: "Look," she said, "They're still there."

AN EARLY CUSTOMER

Alfred's first customer had already turned up before the store even opened. Alec Hamilton lived across the street and saw that there might be a new store, so he came over, even though there wasn't a single indication, like a sign behind the window, as to what it would be. As Hamilton recounts to Abecassis, he entered the store and saw a man hunched over a coffee roaster.

"It was Alfred Peet, and I asked him, 'What's this place going to be?' In a thick accent, he answered, 'we're going to sell coffee, tea, and spices.'" Hamilton happened to be out of Darjeeling at home, so he asked Alfred if he could buy some. "He sold me a packet although the official opening wasn't until the next day."

When the store opened on April 1, 1966, Alfred immediately started roasting coffee. "Freshly roasted" was his mantra after all, which is also why he preferred to roast coffee in small amounts. Pretty soon, the fire department was knocking on the door. They had been alerted by the neighbors, who were worried about smoke coming out of the store. Unroasted coffee beans have a thin outer layer that gets shed during the roasting, and, with the Royal #5 roaster, those peels went straight into the fire, creating a lot of smoke. Whether this contributed in any way to Alfred's unique style of roasting is up for speculation, as later, he would use a number of different roasters. At any rate, roasting with this kind of roaster was a somewhat risky business in a predominantly wooden building.

It didn't take long for the smell of newly roasted beans to generate curiosity, which was exactly Alfred's intention. On the Peet's blog, one can read the memories of customers who, in the late sixties, saw Alfred in action with that coffee roaster. Their stories make it obvious that they were attracted by the heavenly smell.

Alfred would later explain to the local paper, the *East Bay Express*, "I offered various teas, about fifteen different kinds of coffee, and a number of blends that I had made myself." He also offered spices, as the original name of the store indicated. His store essentially focused on taste and, at that moment in time, America was not exactly clued in to "taste," according to Alfred. "Everyone used percolators and boiled the hell out of the coffee."

"It was a battle to educate customers," Alfred once noted. That said, he did understand why most customers were so uneducated: "If you are used to drinking Hills Brothers coffee and then try Peet's, roasted darker and brewed twice as strong, you wouldn't say it was terrific. It was written all over their faces—'My God, is he trying to poison me?'" Alfred even overheard someone else exclaim one day, "I can't drink this stuff. It's like ink."

One particular group of customers, though, was immediately en- thusiastic, and those were the faculty and students who had come to Berkeley and San Francisco from all over Europe. "People from the university who traveled widely and the people with foreign accents said, 'At last we can have coffee like we remember!'" Alfred recalled.

Convincing customers of the quality of his coffee was some- thing that Alfred did with patience and pleasure, but he could also be blunt. With a booming voice, he'd scold customers about the way in which they made their coffee. Archer remembered an exchange with a woman who came to complain about a broken coffee pot. According to Alfred, she herself was to blame, and he refused to refund her. "She then hit him over the head with the coffee pot." Archer had to laugh, remembering it, and added that Alfred wasn't hurt by the incident.

THE CLASSIC BLEND

One of Alfred's first customers was Bonnie Grossman, who ran an art gallery down the street from the store. She witnessed how one of the most popular coffees at Peet's came into existence. The idea for this coffee was given to Alfred by a customer, former Sergeant Key Dickason, with whom Grossman used to drink coffee. "Key had very firm opinions about coffee. His suggestions made Alfred compose a blend and name it after him." In the process, Alfred decided to give the sergeant a promotion and called this top seller Major Dickason's.

The store used to be much smaller than it is now, Grossman told me when I visited her in her house near Peet's. "The space that has the little museum now wasn't part of it. The counter was extended all the way to the front of the shop, and there you could taste coffee." The store had futuristic coffee makers, and the menu was like a trip around the world with references to Indonesia and Guatemala. Grossman said that later they added a bench outside where people could drink their coffee, but most of the coffee drinkers would mill about on the sidewalk or take up part of the street.

Alfred didn't actually intend for the store to be a place where people could come and drink their coffee. He wanted to sell beans, so people could make their coffee at home, but he was afraid that customers would make his higher quality and more expensive beans the wrong way. "I thought, if they buy it from me and take it home and ruin it, they'll say, 'Why should I pay him more money for this?' So, I put in a coffee bar—I let them taste it and talk about it." There were only a few chairs near the bar, and they didn't have backs, which was on purpose, Grossman remembered. The message was clear: Wanting to taste was fine, but customers should not think they could loll about, as one would in a café.

But the customers had a different opinion about that. They used to line up before the store opened, and once inside, they would take the time to enjoy their coffee. They would then linger in the store, which was quickly gaining in popularity. So, Alfred decided to take away the chairs altogether, but the customers remained standing, with coffee in hand, or they would walk outside, where there was a constant crowd.

Hippies, who had also discovered the store, couldn't care less whether there were chairs or not. "They thought my place was groovy, and they simply sat down on the floor," Alfred recalled to Mark Pendergrast, author of *Uncommon Grounds*. "Customers had to step over them, and some of them smelled bad." It bothered Alfred because he wanted to run a "respectable" store, and while he "didn't want to battle" his customers, he'd sometimes get fed up and chase the lingering crowd out of the store.

It may seem trivial, but the dress code at Peet's spoke volumes about the difference between the owner of the store and his customers. The picture of Alfred and the coffee roaster is indicative of how the owner usually dressed: shirt, tie, and shopcoat, like the ones grocers used to wear. When looking at that picture, you wouldn't guess that his was one of the hippest coffee stores in the San Francisco Bay Area at the end of the sixties. To locals, Alfred looked like a technician in a lab, even though his way of dressing was quite the norm for small shop owners in the Netherlands in the fifties.

Alfred expected the same immaculate standard of dress from his employees. "When someone showed up for work in a wrinkled shirt, he'd send him to me, to iron the shirt," said Archer, who lived near the store at the time. In essence, Alfred tried to emulate the classic Dutch coffee stores.

Alfred appeared to present an image of a completely self-educated professional who seemed obsessed with improving himself constantly in order to deliver quality. But that wasn't the full truth. He had learned the profession in the Netherlands, from his father and his uncles, who were also in the business. He wouldn't renounce that background and experience per se, but he did seem to have embraced the American pioneering mythology, and even Americanized his middle name, changing "Henri" to "Henry."

Above all, the way in which he managed the store, his focus on Indonesian coffee, and his Dutch directness made him stand out in the Bay Area. And that was a good thing. To Americans, both his customers and other coffee entrepreneurs, he was seen as a coffee connoisseur from the Old World, and thus he seemed much closer to the roots and history of coffee and its culture.

Alfred's customers weren't bothered by the somewhat eccentric mentality and temperament of the founder. The classic European charisma of the shop boosted the appeal of Peet's. It was almost exotic to find such a store on the West Coast, with a coffee guy from faraway Holland who, for whoever wanted to see it, turned raw, green beans into a heavenly black brew.

HIPPIES AND COFFEE

When Alfred opened his store, the era of "flower power" and "going to San Francisco with flowers in your hair" was in full swing. Around the San Francisco neighborhood of Haight-Ashbury, a music culture emerged with bands such as Jefferson Airplane and the Grateful Dead. Elsewhere in the city, Sly Stone developed his revolutionary mix of soul, funk, and psychedelic rock. The Civil Rights Movement was coinciding with protests against the Vietnam War, but despite potential upheaval, things were relatively peaceful in the liberal city of Berkeley.

Politically, the sixties didn't impact Alfred on a personal level, even though his contemporaries (people in their late forties) were swayed by the times. Alfred remained entrenched in his conservative, Catholic upbringing, staying true to his Dutch roots from his hometown of Alkmaar. That would change later, because he couldn't remain entirely immune to this milieu, and interestingly, if some of his more left-wing customers liked to challenge the more conservative Alfred, they did so respectfully. Such was the relationship Alfred shared with his customers.

Archer remembered a man by the name of John Paul who seemed to make it a point to get thrown out of the store. She saw him arrive one day, and he seemed to be planning on getting kicked out again. "He always wore a hat in the style of Captain Hook. It had a large feather and, that day, he had a bunch of garlic wrapped around his neck. John Paul took his shirt off and Alfred took prompt action. 'Man, put some clothes on. This is a store!' he said." But that was it—that was the extent of his attempt to get this customer thrown out.

There were other notable customers. The neighbor across the street, Hamilton, remembered a coffee aficionado with a live Boa constrictor around his neck. "Even though it was a nice friendly beast, he was asked not to come in—the snake was scaring customers away."

Hamilton also remembered how the store was often overrun. There were always people gathered at the corner, making it look as if there were an event going on. The term "Peetnik" to describe Peet's fans was quickly coined, apparently thought up by local police officer Don Clendenen. Customers started using the term to be included into the group of connoisseurs who drank Peet's exclusively. No other coffee was up to snuff. With the introduction of the word "Peetnik," it became clear that drinking quality coffee constituted not only a consumer choice, but joining a following and finding a place in the new community that was forming around this store and its product.

In the book celebrating the twenty-fifth anniversary of Peet's, Officer Clendenen remembered how in the beginning bags of beans lay stored against the walls of the store, and coffee was served in porcelain cups. "Outside it was a laid-back corner . . . you could take time to relax and make friends . . . it was time out of your day . . . it was a big social place to get together." Clendenen, too, had to get used to the dark brew of the Dutchman. "At first the coffee was overpowering. I thought this isn't coffee, this is thick mud. But when you go and get hooked on Peet's, you've got to get everyone else hooked on it."

George Howell, a later pioneer of American specialty coffee, also caught the Peet's bug, becoming known for his business Coffee Connection, which was eventually bought by Starbucks. Howell became famous for wanting to improve coffee quality by giving coffee farmers a larger share of the harvest. Howell was quoted on Coffeegeek.com in 2005 as saying, "I was living in Berkeley, and I was driving in 1968 past the original Peet's . . . and I saw all these people standing outside. It looked like a party around two o'clock in the afternoon, with people holding these very interesting porcelain cups with long stems. Paper cups didn't exist at that time."

Howell parked his car, walked inside, and ordered a cup of coffee. "It was a bit on the dark roast side, I didn't know and I wouldn't describe it back then that way, but in any case, I was fascinated. The inside of the Peet's store was amazing. It was like walking into some ancient chemical lab from a fourteenth century or something, with a smell of coffee just permeating the whole store."

CLASSICAL MUSIC

From the first day, the music that was played at Peet's was classical, which was Alfred's favorite music. But if he was out, the music would be changed, according to Mariette Merle, Alfred's niece, who was studying in San Francisco. "If he wasn't here, they'd play trendy rock music. People would be on the lookout, and they'd warn the people inside if they saw Alfred's car. Everything was put back into the order he wanted for his store."

By this time, when Merle was visiting her uncle, the atmosphere had changed in the Bay Area. The carefree ambiance of the Summer of Love of 1967 had lingered, but turmoil on the UC Berkeley campus seemed to indicate that the "flower power" period had come to an end.

In 1969, the students and residents of Berkeley protested against the plans for a park near the university. The resistance turned into a broader protest movement, with the demands of the civil rights activists and the call to end the war in Vietnam. Ronald Reagan, governor of California at the time, eventually mobilized the National Guard to deal with the protesters and vacate the area. In the confrontation that came to be known as "Bloody Thursday," shots were fired, a student was killed and dozens were injured among both protesters and the police.

Alfred had no real affinity with the protest movement. All he cared about was his store. "I'll leave Berkeley as soon as they smash in one window," he warned the people around him. When he was called one night and told that a window had indeed been smashed in, he hurried to his store. It turned out to be an accident: A car had hit a utility pole and the pole had smashed through the window.

GOURMET GHETTO

The crowds in front of Peet's were an inspiration to other entrepreneurs. The store's success indicated that there was a hidden demand for artisan products with better flavors. A little over a year after Peet's arrival, a cheese shop opened nearby. The Cheese Board offered French and other European cheeses, as well as local ones. Throughout his life, Alfred was always very supportive of entrepreneurs like himself, so when the founders of the Cheese Board, Elizabeth and Sahag Avedisian, opened their store, Alfred welcomed them with the words, "You're going to make it!"

In addition to the Cheese Board, other companies began to open: the Produce Center (fruit and vegetables), Cocolat (chocolates), and Pig by the Tail (a charcuterie). It wasn't long before the neighborhood was assuming the nickname the Gourmet Ghetto, a place where foodies could have their fill.

Quality foods that were produced locally became a rallying cry for this new (and by now international) food movement. And after the arrival of Alice Waters's restaurant Chez Panisse in 1971 (around the corner from Peet's), the neighborhood became a place of pilgrimage for lovers of locally produced organic food.

Alice Waters had also come to Berkeley for Peet's coffee, and she immediately saw the potential. "Peet's and the Cheese Board absolutely had an impact on the neighborhood," Waters said in the aforementioned Peet's publication. "I knew Mr. Peet, and his shop was a fantastic gathering place. When I started my restaurant . . . I picked a location on Shattuck Avenue. It definitely was the commercial place to be." Just as Alfred became the pioneer for specialty coffee, Waters became one of the leaders of the organic (and local) foods movement, as a cook, author, and activist.

The appeal of locally grown organic foods didn't come out of left field. Part of the counterculture in San Francisco (especially hippies) in the late sixties focused on nature and food, and many moved from the city to the country to grow their own food. Markets sprang up where these foods were sold. The story of small-scale production was reinforced in 1971, when a report by the Club of Rome warned that the earth's resources would be depleted quickly if we didn't intervene. But, political timeliness aside, the main priority for many people who came to the Gourmet Ghetto and encountered this movement was simply to seek out good food, which the neighborhood now supplied in abundance.

Undoubtedly, Alfred must have been very happy with the trek of foodies to North Berkeley. The shops didn't compete with each other per se, and together they made the neighborhood all the more attractive. Alfred liked good food, too, and, according to his friends, he was a good cook. His interest in spices seems to have underscored that, and the rise and popularity of the Gourmet Ghetto must have been a source of joy for Alfred.

"Organic" became a buzzword in the United States in the beginning of the seventies. It also stimulated similar movements in other countries where classic outdoor markets became part of the street landscape, and influenced the recent rise of the so-called "food halls." This phenomenon, which has European roots and has been enjoyed in Southern Europe for centuries, can be seen today in the Ferry Building in San Francisco. For more than twenty years, local producers have presented their products inside and outside of the building, and there's a food market full of restaurants that serve California cuisine. You can also drink coffee there—Peet's was the first coffee business to open a shop there.

"Listen to the beans; they will let you know when they are ready."

—Alfred Peet

2

BETTER THAN THE REST

hen Alfred started up his Royal #5 coffee roaster for the first time in his Berkeley shop, he launched something very special. He restored the flavor of coffee in the United States by showing his customers what it was supposed to taste like.

Designer David Lance Goines, who arranged the typography for the first Peet's, described this coffee revolution by contrasting Alfred's products with the coffee his grandfather drank: Folgers coffee, from a can, with half of his mug filled with condensed milk. "It smelled really good. . . . but it didn't have much of a taste," Goines said, "A cup of Peet's coffee has the full, velvety thickness, the mouthfeel, that the fragrance promises. Peet's coffee is coffee that tastes like coffee smells."

The "wretched" quality of coffee in the United States was something Americans had gotten used to during World War II. Coffee was scarce in those years and on the front there was an entire generation of young men who, on a daily basis, drank a tasteless coffee surrogate, which was nonetheless a welcome diversion from the ongoing battle. After the war, it took a while to get the supply of quality coffee going, but people's taste buds had changed so much that there was no real demand for better—and more expensive—coffee.

Add to this the "free refill" phenomenon of American restaurants, and one can imagine that coffee companies didn't see a need to improve the quality. Worse than that, they started roasting coffee lighter and lighter, steadily decreasing the quality of the final brew to increase profits. A lighter roast can make the flavor come out better if done correctly, but the kind of roasting these companies were doing at the time was purely intended to prevent weight loss of the beans and thus increase revenues.

Of course, there were people who tried to go against the mainstream even before Alfred opened his store in Berkeley. And there were many others who would do so after he opened his shop. But none of them had quite the same, unique impact Alfred had.

Through the Italian community, espresso had gained some ground in the United States, and local roasters—most notably Graffeo, in San Francisco—started delivering beans for espresso to cafés and restaurants. But there wasn't the kind of coffee culture that Alfred established. Coffee was merely a drink one had at breakfast or after dinner, and even with espresso, very few knew or cared about the origin of the beans.

Some tried to generate attention for the different kinds of coffee and coffee-making methods and encouraged people to make coffee at home with quality beans rather than using coffee from a can. Capricorn Coffees (which still exists today) had been trying to elevate the coffee experience in San Francisco since 1963. The founders were coffee lovers, but their shop may have been more of a side business than a primary enterprise, considering that one of the founders later became a prominent judge in the city.

Herbert Hyman, founder of the Coffee Bean & Tea Leaf from Los Angeles, walked a similar path as Alfred's. Sometimes he and Alfred are seen as the two major innovators of the new coffee culture in the United States.

In addition, the influential coffee businesswoman Erna Knutsen of Knutsen's Coffee deserves a mention here as well. She coined the term "specialty coffee" and is known as the grand lady of the movement in coffee appreciation. Knutsen was also a trailblazer for other women, since the coffee world had always been dominated by men.

The aforementioned George Howell, who was inspired by Peet's and then started the Coffee Connection in Boston, also became a significant name in the American coffee world. He became known for his emphasis on sustainability and fair trade practices in the countries that produced coffee.

DEMANDING BETTER COFFEE

From the beginning, Alfred always told himself he had to be better than the rest. However, coffee traders in the United States treated him as a regular customer and tried to sell him ordinary coffee. It was business as usual for them, but not for Alfred. "My hair stood on end from that. 'That's exactly the coffee that I don't want. If I sell that, I'm just like the rest,' I told them. I had to do it better . . . otherwise, I wouldn't have the right to exist," Alfred said.

Without that exceptional ambition and drive, Alfred wouldn't have been so influential. Everyone who worked with him noted that they didn't know of anyone else who had such high standards. He insisted on maintaining a thorough knowledge of coffee variety, the quality of the beans, the roasting of the coffee, the way to prepare it, and the best ways to present and explain it to the customer. He was involved in every aspect of the process, and everything had to be done in accordance with his high standards.

But Alfred wouldn't have made it without his natural talent, either. In the American coffee business, he was far above others due to his gift for tasting coffees (known as cupping), his uncanny ability to name them, and his talent for combining them into blends. No one was better than Alfred Peet, say the people who worked with him. He had learned a lot from his father, who had a coffee store in the Dutch town of Alkmaar, but without a dogged devotion to and development of this gift, he wouldn't have reached the high level for which he was praised.

Alfred became influential because he could convince others to adopt his approach to coffee, and he was prepared to put time into that endeavor. He spent hours and hours explaining to his customers what was so special about his coffee. In the same way, he taught other roasters the profession, and he helped many entrepreneurs set up their businesses. His readiness to share his know-how with his peers and develop the market seems almost like a prequel to the way in which the Silicon Valley later developed its talent and morphed into a technological powerhouse.

And then there was Alfred's trademark: The dark roast. Whoever tasted Peet's coffee for the first time had to get used to the dark, bold roast, but after that, people were sold. There was something addictive about it for coffee drinkers on the West Coast who were used to the inferior quality of coffee and its light roast. In the seventies, employees of Peet's in Berkeley sometimes referred to their store as "the opium den" when observing the lines outside, before the store opened its doors.

Starting at the end of the sixties, the dark roast gradually spread all over the United States—all thanks to Alfred. But what was his secret recipe?

A WAREHOUSE FULL OF COFFEE

Even before Alfred opened his business, he had already purchased large amounts of coffee, which he stored in a warehouse in San Francisco. At any given moment, there were between fifteen to twenty 150-pound bags. Green coffee beans can be stored for quite some time, but after a year their quality starts to degrade. The large supply certainly gives the impression that Alfred was convinced he'd succeed.

The reason he filled a warehouse first was because he felt that he couldn't open a store and then go look for coffee. As Alfred put it, "Coffee was the first thing I needed. I could have roasted the coffee in a warehouse and could have sold it everywhere, even from my house, as long as people knew where they should go to get it." Another important reason for storing so much coffee was that good quality beans were still quite scarce in the United States.

Alfred didn't always find what he wanted with American vendors, and the export of his favorite Indonesian coffee from the Netherlands had slowed down. After the Indonesian National Revolution (1945–1949), Indonesia didn't want to sell any more beans to the Netherlands, but during a visit to Germany, Alfred heard about a coffee company in Hamburg that could deliver from both Java and Sumatra. He inquired with the Dutch embassy in Hamburg and was referred to the trader List & Beisler.

Hans-Dieter Mallasch, one of the founders of List & Beisler, worked there when Alfred arrived at the renowned coffee company. As Mallasch explains, "It was 1967 when he came here for the first time. We decided to taste coffee for three days, and it immediately struck me that we had the same ideas." Together with Alfred, he tasted coffees from Kenya, Guatemala, Costa Rica, Indonesia, and Papua New Guinea. "We had an ample supply, and he was really happy that he had found us," says Mallasch.

Alfred, on the other hand, felt he was being tested. "The people who were present seemed to assess what I was made of. When you taste coffee, you'll know after five to six minutes." Needless to say, Alfred passed his "exam."

Mallasch told Alfred that all Indonesian coffees in Europe were transported via a representative in Hamburg whom he happened to know. "Nowadays, everyone can have access to coffee farmers but back then it wasn't easy," Alfred commented later. "In the coffee trade, it's all about personal contacts, much like the diamond trade. That makes it so special—I love it."

Mallasch remembered Alfred as a "hard man" when dealing with the quality of coffee. "He expected clear answers. But later he trusted us. When we told him the quality was good, he'd buy it. He didn't do that with everyone." Wolfgang Dehner, cofounder of List & Beisler, commented that Alfred was his favorite customer. "He was by far the most interesting person I've met in the coffee world. He had precise ideas about what he wanted and couldn't be swayed otherwise. He was very decent all around and very reliable." Alfred made sure he didn't lose the Germans' trust, saying, "They sent containers with coffee with the invoice included. If they really trusted you, you'd hurry to pay that bill."

Mallasch and Dehner both became friends with Alfred after that first meeting. Dehner visited him in the Bay Area several times with his wife, and he got to see some of Alfred's private life, which he didn't reveal to many. At the same time, Alfred was more than just a friend: He helped the Germans get a foothold in the American market. Starbucks became a client of theirs, too. To this day, List & Beisler delivers coffee to Peet's, continuing a collaboration that goes back more than fifty years.

When buying coffee, Alfred was always looking for the best quality, as Mallasch and Dehner knew; but if the price of a certain coffee had risen too much, he'd look for other beans. An employee of Peet's once saw that he ignored a cargo of Kenyan AA-type beans for that very reason. Customers won't pay that price, Alfred explained. So he turned to other Kenyan beans with the same quality but at a lower and more acceptable price.

WHICH COFFEE?

Coffee beans are by no means all alike. Certain features of the beans surface as soon as a coffee roaster starts roasting. Alfred once talked about the effect of altitude on beans: "You can compare coffee beans to wood. Beans that grow at a high altitude are hard, dense, and are more like oaks. Those beans need more heat while roasting."

Coffee comes from two main varieties of beans: arabica and robusta, with a multitude of variations among them. The arabica (*Coffea arabica*) originated in Ethiopia, and its main variation is Typica. But there are dozens of others, such as Gesha/Geisha (also from Ethiopia), Mundo Novo (from Brazil), and SL-28 (from Kenya).

When a farmer chooses a plant, the quality of the coffee is one factor, but location where he wants to grow is also important. Some plants are more suitable for high altitudes, and when there are plant diseases like leaf rust, the farmer may resort to variations that are more resistant to that. Trends also play a role. For example, the Panamanian Geisha coffee has been very popular in the last few decades, so enthusiasm (and demand) for that plant will increase.

After the harvest of the coffee beans, the farmer has to make another important decision: How is the coffee flesh extracted? Worldwide, two methods are used. In several countries, coffee farmers put the coffee beans out in the sun to dry (natural or dry processing). The berries are turned over regularly to dry them evenly and prevent problems like mold. Because the flesh stays in contact with the beans for a long time, the coffee obtains more of a fruity flavor.

But coffee beans can also undergo wet processing. This is more common because it leads to more consistency in quality and higher acidity (an indicator of freshness); coffee connoisseurs claim that, in this way, the character of the coffee bean becomes more pronounced. With the help of a so-called depulper, the flesh of the berries is removed, which is followed by a period of fermentation, during which the pulp is still in contact with the beans. Then the coffee beans, which contain thin papyrus type peels or skins, are dried. This can happen either naturally outside or in dryers made for coffee beans. The amount of time for every step can vary and this influences the taste of the coffee as well.

HEAT, SMOKE, AND FIRE

Alfred once said, "As opposed to tea, coffee is not a ready-made ingredient. You've got to do something with it." He was referring to roasting, and roasting is truly a fascinating process to watch, so it's not too surprising that Alfred placed the roaster in full view of the customers. Even modern roasters still look like machines that seem to go back to the Industrial Revolution. When beans are being roasted, there is heat, smoke, fire, and noise. Hatches open and close. Big bags of green beans, feeling like rubber to the touch, are being dragged to the roaster.

The work usually starts early in the morning, as the machines have to be preheated properly. There is an optimal moment to drop the beans into the machine via a funnel. That moment depends on the kinds of beans. For example, the Harar beans from Ethiopia will have a different "drop temperature" than Antigua beans from Guatemala.

Once the roaster has been turned on and the beans are in, the roastmaster starts a game of heat and air, during which the beans are roasted. Gradually, the heat transfers to the beans themselves and the container in which the beans are spinning around. So, there are three elements that have to be balanced, and on top of that, the weather outside also plays a role.

"On a cloudy day, the roaster responds differently than when you've had long periods of warmth and dry air," Alfred explained once. "That's more problematic than when the air humidity is higher. There's a lot of air that goes through the roaster, so the quality of that air makes a difference."

During the roasting, the roastmaster checks the progression by using a built-in scoop to retrieve small amounts of beans from the gyrating roaster. In the meantime, the beans swell, and then there is a sudden popping, like popcorn, the moment at which the moisture inside the beans gets expelled with some force. It depends partially on the temperature and the beans, but usually this happens around ten minutes after the beans have been dropped into the roaster.

After the first pop, the beans are almost ready to be taken out because from that point you'll have drinkable coffee. But depending on the desire of the roastmaster, a second pop will follow. The second pop is less loud, but the oils of the beans will be pushed to the surface. The roastmaster has to be very careful now. The risk of burning the beans is very high at this point. The coffee will then taste like coal or have a burnt flavor and be completely undrinkable.

Alfred was a master of dark roasts, which means he went beyond the second pop without losing the characteristic features of the coffee. In his dark roast, he achieved a remarkable balance of acidity, mildness, and fullness of flavor (also known as "body"). Followers of Alfred who tried to emulate this type of roasting noticed how difficult it was. Many would burn their beans.

How do you determine the moment when you have to take the beans out of the roaster? "The coffee will speak to you and will let you know when she's ready," Alfred told his students. For outsiders this sounds mystifying, but those who wanted to learn the profession from him developed an ear for it as well.

Alfred refined the style he had known from the Netherlands, from his father and from his uncles who were in the coffee business, too. The darkest varieties for coffee roasting are originally European, like the French roast and the Italian espresso, but Alfred had also seen dark roasts in a different place, and that was Indonesia.

"They roasted the beans very dark over there. In the morning, you needed a hit over the head. After you had been perspiring in your bed all night, you wouldn't feel rested until you had had your coffee. That's why I roasted it somewhat darker here as well. American colleagues were surprised and said, 'you can sell that stuff!'" he said in the eighties in an interview with the Dutch newspaper, *NRC Handelsblad*. The same journalist saw how Alfred made the coffee himself and was surprised by the simplicity of the coffee guru's method. "He pours boiling water on some freshly ground beans. Then he pushes the grounds to the bottom. That's it. His coffee is pretty damn strong, as was to be expected. The secret, however, is in the beans."

For a perfect roast, you wait for the right moment to take the beans out, and when the moment finally arrives, you pull a handle to drop the freshly roasted beans into a container where they can cool off quickly. It's a glorious sound when the roasted coffee falls into that container. If you buy beans and you drop the beans in a container at home, you'll know the sound, but in a coffee roaster it is amplified many times over. It's an appropriate closing note.

"Often, I see one of our roastmasters throw up his arms and call out, 'Oh, how hard it is to roast coffee!' And I can only confirm that," Alfred acknowledged later, after years and years of experience. Alfred was already a consultant then, and the coffee roasting was done by others. "The roastmasters," he said "are the most important people in my company. These people can make or break me. I can buy the best coffees, but during the roasting, that quality will come out or not. Talented roastmasters will keep the company going. Day in, day out."

"There was always something going on with him."

—Gertrude van der Flier-Peet, Alfred's sister

3

GROWING UP WITH COFFEE IN A CHEESE TOWN

he reason Alfred started his business in the United States had largely to do with a failed succession in the family business, thousands of miles away, in his Dutch hometown of Alkmaar. In Alkmaar, a town not too far from Amsterdam that is mostly famous for its cheese, Alfred's father had a thriving coffee business. The plan had been that Alfred would succeed his father. This didn't happen, and it begs the question: What would have happened if Alfred hadn't moved abroad?

It's likely that he would have become one of the many Dutch roasters who, in the second half of the last century, were forced to go out of business, due to competition with large supermarket chains. It's doubtful that Alfred would have tolerated working with his father, as the relationship between the two was not a bed of roses.

A DIFFERENT PATH

Alfred's father was supposed to become a priest. The son of an Amsterdam butcher, Henri Peet was born in 1879 and had been schooled by the Jesuits in the city of his birth. Why he exchanged church ritual for the rituals of a coffee roasting company is not entirely clear. He certainly had not left the faith, as he remained a devout Catholic for the rest of his life.

After leaving the Jesuits, Henri was sent to Alkmaar by his parents. "They had heard that there was a coffee business for sale there and thought it might be a suitable profession for their son," explained Gertrude van der Flier-Peet, Alfred's older sister, who was interviewed in Wassenaar in 2014. She was ninety-seven then, but the memories returned as she talked, and she spoke with a resolve that was also typical of her younger brother Alfred.

It was unusual for a butcher's son to go into coffee. But apparently his parents knew this world well, since they became aware of a coffee business for sale in Alkmaar. It's highly likely that Henri Borghols, Henri's brother-in-law and coffee merchant, played a role in this. This is evident not only because of his business connections, but also because of the capital that was put up to finance the purchase of the coffee business B. Koorn & Co in Alkmaar.

With the acquisition of this locally known store, Henri obtained two centuries-old buildings on the Fnidsen, a small industrious street in the center of Alkmaar. The house at number 119 had already been a residence with a shop in 1744. At that time, it had been owned by a silversmith, but in subsequent years, it turned into a linen store and then a grocery business.

For the owner Bernardus Koorn, there was only one reason to sell his thriving coffee store: He had no successors. For almost an entire century, the coffee and tea business on the Fnidsen had been in the hands of the wealthy and influential Koorn family. The place had a great reputation and, wisely, Henri preserved the name when he acquired the shop. In contrast with the previous owners, who had described themselves as merchants in colonial goods, Henri called himself a "coffee roaster and merchant" from the start. Significantly, even though he also sold tea, he made it clear that freshly roasted coffee was his priority, and, if you walked past his store, the aroma made that more than clear.

CITY OF SMALL INDUSTRIES

Due to industrialization, Alkmaar was going through a boom when Henri started as a coffee entrepreneur. At the beginning of the twentieth century, large companies, such as a butter factory, emerged in town. Yet the emphasis was on the smaller industries in Alkmaar and the city's culture exuded that focus. "One can easily walk in the middle of the street and have a chat. The only thing that you may notice is a handcart with a horse," Alkmaar resident H.J. De Graaf later wrote about the turn of the century, "The paving of roads is an unknown phenomenon here. But there are stoops alongside the homes. Especially in the Langestraat one will see these, cordoned off by stoop chains, which children may use as a swing."

Henri sold his coffee from his shop on the Fnidsen, but he also sold to larger companies in the city and the region, as well as hotels and restaurants. In addition, there were resellers who would sell his coffee door to door in Alkmaar and the surrounding area.

The young businessman was completely in his element in Alkmaar. From the ads he placed in the regional newspapers, you can tell he was confident and eager to win customers. Whether he wrote the copy himself remains unknown, but he must have controlled the content and approved the tone of the ads. Where others from coffee companies in Alkmaar merely described what they had for sale, what it might cost, and where the location of the store was, Henri explained why you had to buy from him. Also, he didn't hesitate to go after the competition. He extolled the artisan quality of his coffee and tea that had been prepared by "experts" with the "utmost care." Because of this, he seemed to argue, they were very different from the mass products one could find elsewhere.

Several years after he had set up shop in Alkmaar, Henri got to know his future wife, Richarda Van den Brink. She was nine years younger and the daughter of an affluent carpet manufacturer from Laren. When they got married in 1916, Henri definitely "married up." One family member would become Secretary of Economic Affairs of the Netherlands. Or as his granddaughter Mariette Merle would later say, "Grandma was a grande dame."

Within his extended family, Henri found another relative who was in the coffee business. His name was Henri Keijzer and he had quite a reputation in Amsterdam. The coffee company of the Keijzer family had been in existence since 1839, and when times were really good, they had fifteen shops. A picture, taken during the company's hundred-year anniversary showed the board of directors and seventy-five employees. In those days, that could be called a coffee empire. For a long time, the family lived on the Herengracht in the so-called "Gouden Bocht" (Golden Bend), a prestigious part of Amsterdam where many wealthy people lived. Henry Keijzer was married but had no children, and thus would have succession problems as well, though they were different from those of his brother-in-law in Alkmaar.

"My uncle had an incredible art collection," Alfred later remembered in a conversation with the author Adah Bakalinsky. "I loved being there. My uncle knew more about tea than my father. I often said to my dad, 'I love your coffee more, but his tea is better.' Uncle Henri sold a beautiful Darjeeling. My father had good tea, but he was much more interested in coffee. That was his first love."

Alfred often played with his sister in Keijzer's coffee store on the Prinsengracht, the most well-known coffee store in Amsterdam.

"Alfred was over the moon when he saw the shop again on the Prinsengracht at the turn of the century," noted someone who was there when he was revisiting the place. "He immediately went behind the counter and wanted to see everything." The name Keijzer is still on the building, but the shop is now owned by Simon Lévelt, another well-known Dutch coffee roaster and merchant.

Two years after his marriage to Richarda, a fourth coffee merchant entered the family, marrying Henri's youngest sister. This coffee merchant also had the name Henri, a coincidence that surprised Alfred. Henri Lindner was a coffee broker in Amsterdam, together with his brother. They delivered green (unroasted) coffee beans to a large number of roasters in the Netherlands and, naturally, if Lindner received an interesting batch of coffee beans, they let Henri know about it in Alkmaar.

BORN AT THE ROASTER'S

The two buildings (shop and residence) on the Fnidsen weren't suitable for Henri's rapidly expanding family, which, when the twenties began, already included two daughters: Gertrude and Mathilde. They also had servants. When, on March 10, 1920, Alfred was born as the first son, it became clear that the family had to move. Alfred lived at the Fnidsen for a year before they moved to the Wilhelminalaan, a street that is especially known for a well-established military academy.

"Finally, a real house," Gertrude, Alfred's oldest sister said. "We proudly told about it in school, but got pitiful glances."

In the Wilhelminalaan and nearby neighborhood, the residents were doctors, architects, or businessmen. It was a different social atmosphere from the Fnidsen, which was distinctly middle class, and in appearance, this new neighborhood was vastly different as well. The Fnidsen was, and still is, a busy, narrow street, whereas the Wilhelminalaan was a quiet neighborhood bordering a wooded nature area where one could hike. Business was good, or so it seemed when the family moved to the formal Wilhelminalaan. It's possible that Richarda influenced the move because she may have wanted to live in an area that was more like her parents' in Laren. For more than four years the family lived there, until Henri bought the beautiful residence on the Kennemersingel, just outside of the city center and across from the most famous windmill in Alkmaar.

After the move to the Kennemersingel, Henri and Richarda became part of the ruling elite of the town. It was clear that they played a prominent role in the city between the two World Wars. Richarda was part of a committee to help the poor and also sat on a committee for the promotion of the singing arts (she sang herself). In addition, she was active in the committee for the "education and relaxation of soldiers living in Alkmaar." Henri became involved in the community, too: He became a regent for the central hospital, which was the biggest hospital in town.

It was in the house on the Kennemersingel that Alfred must have witnessed the family parties of the coffee businessmen and uncles (the aforementioned Henris) who could talk about their profession for hours. After that, the topic of conversation became wine. Henri wasn't particularly fond of the wine choices of his brother-in-law who was a wine merchant. Gertrude remembered how her father once took a bottle, which his brother-in-law had praised, to the canal behind the house and made a point of emptying it into the canal. Alfred would come to share his disdain for most of his American coffee colleagues in much the same outspoken way.

THE SMELL OF COFFEE

On the Kennemersingel, Alfred got his first taste of coffee. As he recalled, "When father came home, he always had bags of coffee in his pockets. They were the newly made coffee blends that he wanted to try out at home. The smell of his coat with the coffee is the strongest memory I have of that time."

Henri brought in the samples to have them judged by his wife so that he could then place his orders with the coffee merchants in Amsterdam. "When my mother reacted in a certain way to the coffee he had brought, he knew that he had to change something," Alfred said. His sister Gertrude remembered clearly how her mother would place a row of cups on the kitchen table for the tasting, which is known as "cupping."

For a coffee merchant and roaster, cupping is one of the most important facets of the profession. The ritual that could be seen at Henri's house is repeated every few days in coffee companies, or even daily. Repeated cuppings and discussion about taste are the only ways to find good coffees, and at the same time, it's also the best method to develop one's taste. Typically, every tasting has an element of suspense and hope, because the discovery of a new coffee can be life changing.

A cupping follows a fixed pattern. A small batch of beans is roasted, ground, and distributed among a row of cups on the tasting table. Smelling the coffee will lead to a first impression. Then hot water is poured onto the coffee, and after some time the coffee surfaces and forms a thick crust on the surface. After a moment or so, the cupper breaks through the crust with a special spoon, capturing a small amount of coffee, which is then slurped up quickly. The slurping is important as it brings in oxygen, which reinforces the flavor of the coffee. Just like a wine taster, a cupper spits out the coffee in a receptacle.

After that, the spoon is cleaned in water, and the cupper proceeds to the next coffee. Experienced cuppers go very quickly from one cup to the next, in search of that one coffee that's unforgettable. During the cupping, one hears slurping and spitting, accompanied by comments, and, now and then, a cry of admiration when there is something special. At a competition where several coffee producers send in their harvest, cupping can take days, and a jury may taste dozens or even hundreds of coffees.

A WELL-DEVELOPED PALATE

Alfred and his sisters were also allowed to taste from the coffees on the table. "We didn't like it at all. But in the Netherlands at the time, the coffee used to be very strong. We always added hot milk to it." When he became a coffee entrepreneur the tasting table became something special for Alfred. "I like my tasting table the best. That's where you can romanticize. You look at your coffees or teas, in your head you can put them together, and at a certain moment, you can see if what you saw in your mind has the effect you planned."

As a coffee entrepreneur, Alfred's father had a well-developed palate, and it became clear that the kids were endowed with that gift as well. Later, Alfred remembered how he and his brother Rudolf used to comment on the dishes their mother put on the table. "The flavors of the food were elaborately discussed, not only when it wasn't good but also when it was tasty. My mother would tire of that sometimes. Poor woman—the things she had to put up with," Alfred laughed.

Alfred couldn't remember the store on the Fnidsen very well. "I do know that I played there and climbed over the coffee bags until my father had enough of it and sent me away. But like a sponge, I did learn several things there about coffee and tea," he recalls. His sister Gertrude remembered how Alfred would help for hours in the business, packaging coffee, saying, "He did enjoy coming there."

Henri Peet first sold coffee based on weight, which was common in those days. Later, however, he added colored labels to his coffees, which indicated quality. There were about twelve different blends, which he had mixed using different beans. This was largely done to offer customers a consistent quality. "The cheapest coffee my father had was made of robusta beans. I didn't care for it much, but it was the best robusta you could get. At home, we didn't touch the stuff—it was coffee for poor people."

According to Alfred, the coffee culture in the Netherlands before World War II revealed a certain class-consciousness. "Everyone belonged to a certain social class and it was hard to escape it. Our social class drank top quality. If you were unemployed, you wouldn't drink what we were drinking—you'd go for the cheaper blends." Alfred concluded that his father basically had a coffee for every social class. "My God, what an awful system," he sighed. But his father wasn't the only one who made these distinctions; other roasters and merchants also showed a variation in quality and pricing. Nowadays, no one is surprised or shocked anymore by the different coffees (from the cheap house brand to the more expensive arabica beans) offered in stores.

"My father was a very good coffee businessman," Alfred said. "He was one of those old-fashioned Victorian types. If it weren't top notch, he wouldn't even bother to talk about it. He was very conservative in the way he worked. When I look back as to how he did it, I would have done it differently. But that was not part of his temperament. For my father, everything had to be 100 percent secure before you started anything. But life doesn't always work out like that. That was the only way he'd approach things—only do things when you're absolutely sure of it. It worked well for him, in his time."

PUSHING BOUNDARIES

From Gertrude's stories it seems that Alfred was rebellious and that he fought often with his father. "There was always something going on with him," she said, looking back on their childhood. In contrast to the other children, Alfred pushed certain boundaries. "My father was very stern in the way he raised us. You had to do what he told you to do, and you couldn't go against it. We were very obedient and did what he told us, but Alfred wasn't like that. He wanted to make his own decisions."

During dinner, the kids would remain silent unless their father or mother asked them something, which was fairly typical in Dutch families at that time. But Alfred would pipe up, and, when he was asked something, he might give "a rude answer." This often resulted in him having to finish dinner in the hallway.

At other times when Alfred had been misbehaving, he'd get sent to the basement. "For my parents, he was a troublesome child. My father was often angry with him." Rebelliousness was part of his character, Gertrude thought, and during his pubescent years that just got worse. "I remember wondering as a child why he was being so difficult."

One family story is that Alfred grabbed an air gun from the shed and sat down against the house to shoot the tulips off their stems. "It was pretty amazing to be a sharpshooter like that. Sometimes he might hit a bird."

Alfred became friends with Sjef van Kesteren, a boy who lived on the Nassaulaan, around the corner from the Kennemersingel. Together, they had a boat, which they used for the canals in Alkmaar. They also went to concerts in the Concertgebouw in Amsterdam, a trip they would make by train and on foot. Sjef would later marry Alfred's sister Hedwig and their friendship would last a lifetime.

It seems that Alfred was academically challenged. He was held back several times and would drop out when he was in his junior year of high school. He was different in that sense compared to his siblings. His parents likely tried to point to his older sister as a role model: She went to college and got two degrees, while Alfred seemed to have suffered from a fear of exams, high expectations, and a lack of motivation.

Alfred himself thought he "could have gone to college." But he added that his father's expectations were too high. "My father put pressure on me to perform. He wanted me to progress faster, but I couldn't. I became blocked, a kind of defense mechanism that was triggered. I didn't become the Peet my father had in mind. And he wrote me off as a . . . ." And then a silence followed that spoke volumes.

Ultimately, Alfred thought his father considered him a failure. "My dad didn't seem to understand why I failed. He didn't consider me retarded and concluded I didn't have the will to succeed."

They never discussed plans for the future, Alfred said. "The only time we did was when I asked him if I could find a job where I could use my hands. 'No,' he said. That is something that others do, was his opinion. That wasn't our kind of work. That was the most intimate conversation I'd ever had with my dad about my future and what I would do with my life. It was very simple for him. He thought: I gave you the opportunity—you should have gone to college if you had wanted it."

The stories that Alfred would later tell his friends in the United States summoned up the image of a stern, almost heartless father. But Alfred also had a professional respect for his dad and did have a few good memories of the stories his father told them when the family walked back from Mass on Sundays.

Henri might have been too rigid, but that certainly wasn't uncommon for that time, Alfred's family said. The recollections of the rebellious Alfred, who was always clashing with his father and eventually moved abroad, is perhaps only one side of the story. Mariette Merle, Alfred's niece, seemed adamant about sharing some nuance, saying, "But he can't say that he had a difficult childhood." Moreover, others in the family remembered Henri as a "sweet grandfather" and "a quiet man."

Alfred's mother seemed to have been a "warm woman" with real musical talent. In the background, she had an important role in the family business. That can be gleaned from the cupping, which Henri organized at home to ask for her opinion. Interestingly, when Alfred broke things off with his father, he kept in touch with his mother. During his later visits home, she would still serve him the prewar coffee with hot milk, even though Alfred had switched to black coffee years before.

TURNING ALFRED INTO A COFFEE MERCHANT

When school became a struggle, Henri and Richarda sent Alfred to a couple of Catholic boarding schools, first in Roosendaal and then Amersfoort. Other siblings also spent some time there, taught by the nuns or the parish. That wasn't unusual for the time, but it seems that Alfred spent more time there than his siblings. He never talked about that period in his life, and Gertrude couldn't recall either how he'd handled those experiences. Clashes could be expected, considering Alfred's character, but maybe his unruliness played a bigger role in Alkmaar because of his father.

In the meantime, Henri decided to involve Alfred in the coffee and tea business. "And that was fine for me," Alfred admitted later. He helped package the coffee and tea and cleaned the roasters in the store on the Fnidsen. In 1939, Henri sent his son abroad for further training. For half a year, Alfred worked at a London tea firm, and after that, he worked for a few months in Germany with a coffee company.

Most of his other training Alfred received by working for a large importer and exporter of coffee in Amsterdam—according to him it was even "one of the biggest firms in Europe." It could well have been the Nederlandsche Handel-Maatschappij (Dutch Trading Company) at the Vijzelstraat in Amsterdam, which had been founded by King William I and had a large share in the import and export of coffee, tea, and cocoa.

"I saw many coffees there," Alfred said. "You started in the division where coffee was being tasted. I used a very small roaster, roasting the samples that would be tasted later. When the big guys were done tasting, I was allowed to try the coffees myself. I learned a lot at that place." His training there lasted between three and four months.

"Alfred received a very good training from my dad," Gertrude said. Henri himself was content with his pupil, or so it seemed later on. Alfred said, "Friends of my parents told me later that my father thought I was a pretty good coffee guy."

WAR

During World War II, the Peet family had to host a German soldier. "He was not a bad guy. He had a wife and child back home,
so he didn't want to be in Alkmaar at all," Gertrude explained.
Henri feared that his well-stocked wine cellar would get emptied by
the Germans, so he hid his bottles by enclosing them behind false
walls. Shortly after the liberation, Gertrude married and the
guests were impressed with the bottles of wine Henri poured at
the wedding.

But for Henri's coffee company, times were tough during the
war. Coffee was scarce and if there was any, it all went to Germany.
At that time, the Dutch drank surrogate coffee, made from the
most unlikely ingredients, like roasted acorns, beets, grains, and
even ground flower bulbs.

Alfred was called up for the Arbeitseinsatz—a forced labor
system in Nazi Germany—but for some time he managed to evade
it. When they did catch him, he was shipped off to Frankfurt to
a factory where a majority of Dutchmen were forced to work.
This must have been near the end of the war, because at the end
of 1944, Alfred is registered in Amsterdam at a Jan Luijkenstraat
address.

"One day in Frankfurt this guy was trying to recruit me to the
Nazi cause. I had a big mouth, and the next day two guys from
the secret police showed up. They had some papers that said I was
'politically unreliable,' and I was reassigned to a factory with a
bunch of French guys."

Alfred had no idea what they were assembling in the factory
("little parts—they never told you what it was"), but the fact that
he was working with machines and that he was creating something

appealed to him. Faraway from his father in Alkmaar, he was finally working with his hands. His enthusiasm for it became apparent, and the other forced laborers became irritated. Rumor has it that they told Alfred that he should not try so hard, lest he boost the German production.

In the labor camp, Alfred learned the importance of maintenance. "I used grease in the machine, not oil, and it plugged up. The guard explained it to me. I never forgot it—preventive maintenance is better than working a machine until it cracks," he once told business magazine *Inc*. But he had forgotten that he had learned that lesson already at his father's where he cleaned the roasters to keep them running smoothly.

After a leave, Alfred didn't return to Frankfurt but went into hiding in an attic of the shed behind his parents' home. He stayed there until the Netherlands was liberated.

The forced labor period did have an impact on Alfred. He saw the bombings and destruction in Frankfurt, and the fear of getting hit must have been very real for the forced laborers. Because of the experience, Alfred was ambivalent about Germans for the rest of his life. Some even say "he hated Germans with a vengeance," and his friends remember that during dinners in the United States, he might jump up during conversations about World War II, exclaiming that "we should never be allowed to forget it."

At the same time, he had a lot of appreciation for the way in which German coffee merchants did business with him, and he preferred to buy German cars like BMWs because he thought the quality was so much better. The German coffee merchants of List & Beisler, who worked with Alfred and considered themselves his friends, said they never noticed his antipathy for Germans.

At the end of 1945, Alfred became engaged. He had met a woman who also lived at the Jan Luijkenstraat; however, they never got married.

According to a family member of Alfred's, the engagement was called off because the woman came from an upper-class family and the prospective groom felt he "couldn't give her the life she was accustomed to." Alfred would say something similar in the United States when people asked about the marriage. He'd say he could only have married her if he had been able to give her the life of her milieu. The class-consciousness that he knew from his childhood in Alkmaar and against which he had rebelled, was apparently hard to shake off.

LONDON

After World War II, Alfred left for London to work with the tea company Lipton, which seemed to seal the fate of the family company in Alkmaar. Shortly before, there may have been talk of a role in the company, which can be concluded from a change in the registration lists of the city—when Alfred returned to Alkmaar he registered as "company manager of a roasting company."

The partnership with his father was not a success. Alfred explained, "My father was still working in the company and there wasn't room enough for two." Couple that with the broken engagement and the enthusiasm in postwar Holland for starting a new life abroad, and it is easy to understand why Alfred left. And because he had lived in London before, the change would not be a difficult one.

"He was partially rebelling against his father, but he was also seeking adventure," Mariette Merle said. "I think he wondered

— *57* —

whether he could spend the rest of his life in Alkmaar. He did have the personality to go abroad," she said. "Alfred was a very cocky guy. He knew exactly what he wanted."

So, Henri Peet was on his own after the departure of his intended heir. Rudy, Alfred's younger brother, was physically not able to run the company, and in those days, it was rare for a daughter to inherit family businesses. It is unlikely that Henri would have allowed it anyway. He seemed to have encouraged them to go to school and seek careers elsewhere.

A sale of the company seemed imminent, but Henri persevered a fairly long time—at a time when coffee companies in the Netherlands like Koorn & Co had to close their doors or be acquired by larger companies. Until his death in January 1959, Henri headed the company in Alkmaar.

Alfred, who had been living in San Francisco for four years, didn't attend his father's funeral. Due to the length of time it took to travel in those days, this wouldn't have been exceptional, but based on other sources, it seems as if he wouldn't have gone anyway. As mentioned earlier, after his departure from the Netherlands, Alfred kept in touch only with his mother. It was abundantly clear that Alfred wouldn't return to lead the family company after his father had died.

Of the four men with the name of Henri—the coffee merchants from the same family who would talk about nothing but coffee during family gatherings—Henri Peet's career may have been the most impressive. He didn't grow up in a family of coffee merchants like Keijzer; he didn't have other jobs like Borghols; he didn't work with a partner, like Lindner. Thanks to a well-developed palate, the butcher's son from Amsterdam had become a prominent coffee merchant in Alkmaar, and he had done so pretty much on his own. Even though Henri bought a thriving business, every entrepreneur knows how difficult it is to remain successful—and Henri kept the coffee store successful for over five decades.

IT STILL SMELLS LIKE COFFEE

At the current location of Koorn & Co, all that's left is the number 119. In its place is a Mexican restaurant. There is nothing to remind one of the former coffee roasting company. The building next door at 117, where Alfred used to climb over the coffee bags as a child, has been torn down and rebuilt.

And yet, in that very street, it still smells like coffee—a new store has opened down the road and across the street where the owner roasts the coffee on-site.

"I can teach anyone to become a great coffee taster in a few months . . ."

—Alfred Peet

4

THE DUTCH IMMIGRANT

lfred Peet was one of the many thousands of Dutch people who left after World War II, in search of a country that might be able to offer more than the fatherland, which had been partially destroyed and depleted by the war.

The government encouraged people to emigrate. "A segment of our population needs to have the courage, just like in previous centuries, to have a future in larger places than our country," the Dutch Prime Minister Willem Drees said in a New Year's speech in 1950. Alfred had no problems with that. He had lived in three countries—and tried and failed to go to Canada—before he settled in the United States in 1955.

It's surprising that Alfred, outside of the Netherlands, tried to survive by using his tea expertise rather than his knowledge of coffee. After the war, he worked at Lipton in London, the world-renowned company that would later be bought by the Anglo-Dutch company Unilever.

There's a telling anecdote about Alfred while he was at Lipton's, about an occasion when he had to assess a batch of tea. He rejected the entire batch because the tea tasted slightly oily. He was the only one who could taste the oil. The tea was favorably priced and the buyers at Lipton's weren't happy that they had to decline the deal because of the Dutchman. Under a different name, they had the tea tasted again but Alfred noticed the oil again and rejected it. Alfred was proven right when an inspection of the ship in which the tea had arrived discovered a leak in the engine, which had allowed the wind at sea to blow the scent of oil across the bags of tea. A layman wouldn't have been able to taste the difference, but it couldn't get past a master taster like Alfred.

TEA SAMPLES

After a short stint in London, Alfred took off for the Dutch East Indies (modern-day Indonesia) for a job as a quality assurance officer at the Tea Office. It was a prestigious and influential government job that had been around for several decades before the war and had been recently reestablished.

The Tea Office published reports about market developments and also wrote about the quality of tea and extraction of tea leaves. But its most important function was the issuing of quality certificates, which plantations could utilize to show the quality of their teas. These certificates also determined the price of a harvest on the markets in Europe.

In Batavia (which is now Jakarta), Alfred assessed countless samples from the tea plantations, and if the quality of any of them seemed off, he'd go to the plantation himself to see what could be done. "It meant tasting, tasting, and more tasting," he'd say later. This happened in Java because it would take too long to send the samples to the Netherlands, and having to report back from the Netherlands would also take too long. "That loss of time would be too expensive, and the long trip would compromise the quality of the tea."

"It was a very interesting job. I got a unique opportunity to experience the tea industry from a completely different angle, in a beautiful country with an amazing culture. It was just too hot for a Dutchman."

It almost goes without saying that Alfred also learned more
about coffee while he was there. He got the opportunity to see first-
hand the beans from Java and Sumatra that he knew so well and had
learned to love in his childhood. But tea was the dominant factor
at this point in his life. Even when the world started perceiving him
as a coffee guru, Alfred remained a great proponent of the nuances
of tea. He may even have been a bigger expert on tea than coffee.
"I've always regretted that tea didn't become a bigger part of my
revenues," Alfred would later say in a conversation with the author
Adah Bakalinsky. At that time, he believed coffee accounted for 80 to
90 percent of his revenues, leaving only 20 to10 percent from tea.

"In essence, tea is a more interesting product than coffee,"
Alfred said. "Tea you can truly compare to wine; there are as many
teas as there are wines, with as many different flavors, colors, and
bouquets. China has an infinite number of green teas. The North
and South of India, Ceylon . . . the tea from all those areas is
completely different. If you put a wine taster next to a tea taster,
their experiences are practically interchangeable.

"In contrast with tea, coffee is a rather coarse product; the
subtle differences that you see in tea, you can't find in coffee. Also,
it's much more difficult to become a good tea taster. I can teach
anyone to become a great coffee taster in a few months, but with
tea that takes much longer."

"If you look at the 360-degree taste spectrum, coffee doesn't
occupy more than 40 degrees, from the lightest to the heaviest,"
Alfred later said in a newspaper interview. "If you taste Ethiopian,
Kenyan, Guatemalan, and Sumatran, one is heavier; one is
lighter; one has more acidity; one is mellower. But they're not
that different—they all have the 'coffee' taste in common. But you

wouldn't compare a light green tea with a heavy, thick Assam tea—it's like comparing a light white wine with a heavy Burgundy."

The flavor of coffee and tea from the same plantation differs every year, due to changes in the weather or production, Alfred explained to Bakalinsky. "But with coffee those differences are less dramatic than with tea. That has to do with the fact that coffee is a fruit in the end. Compare it to an apple tree of which the apples taste about the same every year. This doesn't apply to tea. The flavor changes when the weather changes. If the leaves absorb a lot of water, there will be very little flavor after the harvest. During the rainy season, you can't grow quality tea. That's why you constantly need tea samples from the plantations to be updated about the condition of the tea."

At that point in the conversation, he couldn't be stopped, and his enthusiasm conveyed his ability to truly inspire others about tea and coffee. Continuing, he said, "During the winter, tea hibernates as it were. During the spring, the first leaves start to grow—the so-called first flush. That's a very refined tea but it has a very fragile flavor. It's something to taste and appreciate in, let's say, a Buddhist monastery. Everything has to be quiet, and focus is required to drink this kind of tea. Anything around can distract from this tea. And you shouldn't eat with it. Go sit on a mountain top to enjoy this tea.

"As a business-minded Dutchman, however, this kind of tea is of little value to me. I wouldn't be able to get enough demand for this expensive tea. It usually gets sent directly to Great Britain and Germany where people may pay $20 to $25 for it, like a good bottle of wine. I usually wait for the second flush—when the dry season has started and the flavor of the tea intensifies."

For Alfred, there was no particular tea that was the "absolute best," although Darjeeling, the tea area in northeastern India, was his favorite. "It has a light character, comparable to the Muscat grape. East of Darjeeling, in Assam, you have tea that's comparable to a good Burgundy. Solid, without being top heavy."

NEW ZEALAND

The situation in the Dutch East Indies became more complicated shortly after Alfred's arrival due to the worsening independence struggle. In 1947, the Netherlands started the first so-called police actions to squash the fight for independence. This struggle would last two years with more than one hundred thousand casualties on the Indonesian side, and more than five thousand victims (including diseases and accidents) on the Dutch side. "It became much more dangerous for the Dutch and British who worked in tea. It became very hard for me to travel across Java," Alfred explained later.

The Netherlands had had the lucrative colony in its possession for centuries, earning handsomely by harvesting spices, coffee, sugar, and tea. "I thought colonialism was a ridiculous concept," Alfred said, in hindsight. "It was so strange to me to go from a cold country to a tropical climate, and then when you get there, tell them what you can and cannot do. It became clear to me very quickly that the Dutch wouldn't stay in Indonesia." When his first contract with the Tea Office came to an end, Alfred decided to leave because of the growing unrest in the country. Alfred expected that if he had stayed, he would have been forced to leave some day. "Instead, I could leave on my own terms."

The next destination was New Zealand where Alfred stayed for about four years. He didn't stay that long because he was having such a good time. On the contrary, he said, "It was a sleepy place.

They have their sheep, cattle, cut wood, and that's it. You're not going to get any heartburn there. I thought the country was too small. There were about two and a half million people at the time, and that isn't enough to develop any economic activity." That was a miscalculation on his part. New Zealand became an important exporter of wool, dairy, meat, and later, wine. New Zealand's varieties of Sauvignon Blanc in particular have earned an international and excellent reputation.

Alfred started with a tea company on the Northern Island in Wellington, but soon decided he wanted to move to a bigger country, like the United States. Obtaining a visa would take two years, but there was another option. To Alfred, it seemed like a good idea to travel to Canada first and, from there, wait for permission to travel to the United States. He quit his job, took a small trip touring New Zealand—and then heard that the Canadian consulate had declined his application.

He was very disappointed, but later he could see the humor of it. "I had applied as a tea taster but that was a profession they didn't need. If I had said that I was a carpenter, they would have flown me in immediately."

So, Alfred had to look for another job. He ended up in a factory where they produced stainless steel, after which he became a sommelier with a hotel, and then worked with a clothing manufacturer in Christchurch, the second largest city in the country. "All these experiences helped me later on," he'd say. "I haven't regretted a single job."

Finally, in 1955, Alfred received a visa to travel to the United States. Most immigrants from Europe landed on the East Coast and would get to see the Statue of Liberty in New York Harbor; but immigrants from Asia, Australia, and New Zealand would land on the West Coast, in the city of San Francisco. Alfred didn't exactly plan on living there, saying, "I settled there for the simple reason that I got off the boat there."

FIRST IMPRESSIONS

Despite his experiences in Indonesia and New Zealand, Alfred didn't board the ship as a seasoned globetrotter. "I was scared to death when I arrived in San Francisco. There you are with your suitcase. You really feel small in such a big country. And you have to start work immediately, because without work, you're in trouble. It was really hard, really very hard, when I look back on it."

That initial period in San Francisco wasn't only hard, it was also confusing. He knew little about the United States or its history. "I had no idea how people would react to whatever I did. It was all very strange." One thing made it easier: Even back then, San Francisco was characterized as one of the most "European" cities in the United States. The streets lined with trees, the streetcars, the liberal and progressive ambiance in the city, and the emphasis on culture—these were things that Alfred recognized and felt at home with.

When he arrived in San Francisco, the Beat Generation had just emerged. Writers such as Jack Kerouac (author of the classic *On the Road*) and the poet Allen Ginsberg were at the center of a counterculture that was primarily based in the Italian North Beach neighborhood. The beatniks (as they were called) rebelled against the staid and conservative fifties and focused on literature (especially poetry) and listened to jazz records by Charlie Parker, Thelonious Monk, Miles Davis, and Sonny Rollins, while being more sexually liberated than the previous generation.

The writers were regulars of the cafés Trieste and Vesuvio. Dark clothing was one of their trademarks, together with sunglasses and an overall sense of cool. Numerous young Americans embraced *On the Road* and traveled cross-country to seek the same adventures that Kerouac had described in his book.

The beatniks were also big fans of coffee, just like their role models and characters from the Beat books. Author William S. Burroughs once said that *On the Road* led to the sale of great quantities of Levi's jeans and a million espresso machines in the United States. But, while coffee seemed in great demand, few people had a true interest in coffee or wondered about the origins of it or knew about its many different flavors. Coffee was merely an accessory, a prop that belonged to the Beat Generation as much as the sunglasses and black turtlenecks.

SELLING BIBLES

In the meantime, Alfred just tried to survive. He lived on Divisadero Street, in the center of San Francisco, and he tried to find work with a tea or coffee company. When that didn't work out, he worked for $30 a week as a salesman in a fashion store for women. It was rare in those days for a male to fill such a job, and Alfred said he was often mocked; but he learned a lot from the owner about management, which gave him the idea that he might start his own business one day.

For a time, he even sold second-hand cars, as well as encyclopedias and Bibles, going door to door. "Selling door-to-door was very hard for me. I was too shy for it. Every time I saw a doorbell, I'd get scared." But while he was doing this, he also managed to work for Freed, Teller & Freed, one of the classic coffee companies in town, with a history that went back to 1899.

At the job agency, Alfred was mostly seen as a tea taster and that didn't increase his chances. Tea and coffee were separate business concerns in the United States back then, which was very different from the situation in the Netherlands. Alfred was advised to go to New York City where he might have better opportunities in tea. But fortunately for the history of coffee, he didn't follow that advice. In the end, he got a job with E.A. Johnson, one of the big importers of coffee in San Francisco.

E.A. Johnson was an important vendor for the large American coffee companies, such as Hills Bros. and Folgers. It's possible that Alfred worked in the coffee roasting facility, due to his experience in his father's shop in Alkmaar. Soon he was to meet the founder of Graffeo, a well-known roastmaster with Italian roots who had a shop in North Beach (which is still there). Graffeo delivered espresso roasts to the Italian community in San Francisco. "He was very secretive about his business and never let me in. He realized I knew more about coffee than he did," Alfred concluded later.

Alfred's own confidence in his knowledge of coffee was paramount to his conclusion that the Bay Area needed a better coffee resource. He was not impressed with the existing coffee companies in San Francisco and often expressed how terrible the coffee was in the city and on the West Coast. One day, he said to a colleague at E.A. Johnson, "I came to the richest country in the world, so why do they drink such lousy coffee?" It would become one of Alfred's most quoted statements in the United States.

In 1965, the cocky Dutchman was fired from E.A. Johnson. This may have been a result of the changes in the coffee market.

Folgers had been taken over by Procter & Gamble, and the new owner closed the San Francisco Folgers office. The market was shrinking. But it's also possible that Alfred was fired for his Dutch directness. To be so critical of what most Americans drank every day was something people might not have appreciated.

FINDING HIS WAY

So once again, Alfred was looking for a job. A few years earlier, he had become an American citizen and, as mentioned before, had modified his name to Henry (instead of Henri). That looked a lot more American, and maybe it was his way of trying to fit in and get a job faster; or maybe he did it to forget about his father.

It's hard to keep up with all the different jobs Alfred had. He even considered becoming a customs inspector. "I love raw materials. It seemed like fun to be in the harbor and inspect all those ships. Or maybe become a customs officer at the airport." Alfred said he passed the test but ended up not being eligible (or high enough on the list) to get hired. And then there was the job as a salesman of hearing aids. Alfred recalls, "I knew too little about it. I need to get out of here, I remember thinking."

It was 1966. Alfred was forty-six years old, and it was more than twenty years since he had left the Netherlands. He didn't have any firm plans for the future, and for the umpteenth time he was looking for a job. But then he had an epiphany: "With everything that I had done since my departure, I realized that my biggest resource was coffee and tea." He had inherited some money from his father so he decided to start his own coffee business. And with that decision, he changed the fate of coffee in the United States, and possibly the world.

"Without a doubt, Alfred was the right person to help us."

—Gordon Bowker, cofounder Starbucks

5

NO STARBUCKS WITHOUT PEET'S

ordon Bowker, one of the founders of Starbucks, remembered the phone call from 1970 as if it had happened yesterday: "Zev called me from San Francisco and said, 'I found the guy. Alfred Peet is our man.'"

Shortly before that, Bowker, Zev Siegl, and Jerry Baldwin had decided to start a coffee shop in Seattle for quality coffee. Siegl was tasked with researching the market for "gourmet coffee" and finding a good vendor for roasted coffee beans. "We needed an interim source of first-rate roasted coffee in order to begin operations," he said. His journey took him to the San Francisco Bay Area and Berkeley.

"We knew absolutely nothing about the roasting of coffee or starting a company," Jerry Baldwin said while speaking to me in San Francisco. "But, in the United States, that doesn't hold you back," he chuckled.

The meeting of Siegl and Alfred Peet was to become the formative event for the intertwined histories of Peet's and Starbucks. There are very few companies that have had such an intimate relationship with a competitor. "Without Peet's, there wouldn't be Starbucks," seems to be the shared opinion among coffee professionals.

In fact, the three Starbucks founders might not have chosen coffee at all for their business model. Baldwin and Bowker met in 1960 at the University of San Francisco and then met up again in

Seattle, Bowker's hometown. Siegl had his roots there, too, where he had studied at the University of Washington. Both Baldwin and Siegl worked in Seattle as teachers, and Bowker wrote articles for a magazine while running an advertising and design company. In the meantime, the three dreamed of starting their own company.

They researched several company ideas and had long talks about it. For a while, they focused on film. Bowker and Baldwin worked on a movie project that never materialized. Bowker also wrote a script with Siegl. "One day, we were having lunch and we realized that we all had bought coffee at different coffee stores," Siegl reminisced. "We looked at each other and talked about the coincidence of that."

But stories of brilliant ideas and how they come about often have different versions, depending on whom you talk to. Bowker believed that the idea for a coffee shop came to him during his drives to nearby Vancouver. He often bought coffee beans there from a tea and coffee shop called Murchie's. "In Seattle and else-where, you couldn't find a single place where you could buy good, freshly roasted coffee beans." The two-and-a-half-hour trip from Seattle to Vancouver took him past Lake Samish where "during one trip, I was blinded by the light that was being reflected off the lake. It was literally like with Paul," referring to the Biblical figure, who, on his way to Damascus, became blind temporarily as a result of a revelation that caused him to change his life drastically. "It came to me right then and there: Start a coffee store in Seattle!"

Bowker knew almost instantly that this would take off. The coffee he poured at home was a hit with his friends, and quickly, the list of orders grew. One day, after buying coffee in Vancouver, US Customs stopped him at the border: "They wanted to know why

I brought so much coffee into the United States. I had about forty pounds of coffee beans in my trunk." For the average American coffee drinker that was a supply for a year and a half.

ALFRED MADE THE LIST

Researching a company in the seventies was a completely different affair from what we're accustomed to now, Siegl explained. "I needed to go to the public library to study dozens of phonebooks, make a list of companies, and start calling people. In this way, you gathered information and if you were lucky, you could make an appointment to come by." Alfred Peet was one of the names on Siegl's list.

Alfred was used to start-up entrepreneurs visiting him. The founder of the nearby cheese shop the Cheese Board had also asked for his advice, and many coffee entrepreneurs from other US cities would head to Berkeley to get lessons from "the Dutch coffee master."

But Siegl had other people on his list, too. For example, in San Francisco, he sought out the well-known coffee store Freed, Teller & Freed but thought that the other companies weren't as interesting. He had looked at Murchie's as well, but their focus was too much on tea, according to Siegl. "In New York City, I went to two companies that always get mentioned when people talk about quality coffee. But their coffee . . . it was useless." But then he walked into Peet's at the corner of Vine and Walnut Streets. "I was completely baffled. I had never seen anything like it. That coffee shop had become such an institution in Berkeley." It was busy, as always, so Siegl immediately noticed the success of the company. He saw how Alfred was selling enormous amounts of beans. "A shop that would deal with such volumes in turnover today would (still) be considered a huge success."

Alfred struck Siegl as "a rigid, somewhat stiff European, but someone who was very well versed in his subject." He suspects that Alfred saw him as a somewhat pushy entrepreneur in the making, who was also slightly brash. Nonetheless, Alfred invited Zev to have dinner at one of his favorite cafés. "That was one of the pivotal moments in my life, and I dare say that it was a crucial moment for the coffee industry in the United States."

Bowker remembered how Zev recommended Alfred as the person with the most knowledge of coffee and the one most willing to share his knowledge. "He called him the most dedicated coffee entrepreneur in the United States. Without a doubt, Alfred was the right person to help us."

But Alfred himself wasn't so eager to connect with a coffee shop in Seattle, which, at that point, only existed on paper. Baldwin explained, "He wanted to know whether we had it in us. That was understandable: Suddenly three guys from Seattle show up without an inch of experience and they want to start a coffee store. He had already built up a good reputation, and his business was taking off."

There may have been other doubts. Alfred was already thinking about a second store in Menlo Park, south of San Francisco, close to Stanford University and what is now Silicon Valley. To branch out as a sort of wholesale supplier for a different coffee shop would have been a distraction for him.

After Siegl's return, the three aspiring entrepreneurs set up a conference call with Alfred to generate interest for their store. Baldwin said, "I still remember we asked him what to call him. 'Well, I think Alfred,' he said. We didn't know then that everyone in Berkeley called him 'Mr. Peet.' Only people who had worked with him in coffee prior to Peet's used more informal terms; he was known then as 'Al Peet.'" The level of informality seemed like a good omen for the three men from Seattle.

Possibly, it helped that Siegl's father was the concertmaster of the Seattle Symphony; or so Siegl speculated. Alfred liked classical music a lot. "But it must have been clear to him, from the contact we had had with him, that we were serious about our plan. At that moment, relatively few people were interested in starting a coffee store. Maybe he was touched by that."

INTERNING

Alfred came with a proposal that he suggested many times over with other coffee entrepreneurs he met: He proposed they become his interns. It was the end of 1970 when the three became Alfred's pupils, right as the winter season began to take off, the busiest time of the year. Bowker was the first one to work in the shop in Berkeley. Alfred shared his knowledge about coffee and the management of his shop. Some of the work was also more mundane, like packing beans, according to Bowker; but just like Siegl, he was very impressed with what he saw in Berkeley. "It was clear that Alfred knew what he was doing. His business exuded authenticity."

Bowker also remembered an important lesson in "selling." Alfred taught him how you could agree with your customers without changing your own opinion. This became clear to him when a woman came running in, pushed a bag of coffee into Alfred's face and screamed at him that the coffee was roasted too lightly. "He looked at her and said, 'I'm sorry it's not what you wanted. Here's another bag of coffee.' I thought it rather rude of her and when she had left, I said that to Alfred. 'Well,' he said, 'I know her. She just received the same bag of coffee.'"

On his way back to Seattle, Bowker met Siegl, who was on his way down to become the second intern. Once again, he traveled home with a trunk full of coffee, but this time it was from Peet's. During the short meeting, he shared with Siegl all that he had learned from Alfred and told him about what he had experienced.

Siegl, who would later be in charge of retail, store development, and tea for Starbucks, was especially taken with the interior of the shop and the exotic names of the coffees. "Alfred had the coolest equipment for making coffee. I remember a European filter machine with which you could make enormous amounts of coffee. Also, the staff members were trained tremendously well." Siegl also found it telling that 85 percent of the retail space was used for the beans and equipment to make coffee. "It signaled that this was a place where you bought beans, to make coffee at home or in the office."

After that, it was Baldwin's turn, and it was also Baldwin who would embrace the Peet's organization the most. He was the only one who had been introduced to the process of roasting coffee and was able to bring the well-known dark roast of Peet's back to Seattle for Starbucks—and ultimately to the rest of the world.

What did Baldwin really learn from Alfred? When he answered that question, you could tell Baldwin used to teach: "To describe what I learned then about the roasting of coffee is like describing what someone learns from a teacher about writing. Roasting coffee is something you have to do over and over. You make mistakes, you learn, you ask questions and you keep doing it to get better at it."

During his internship, Baldwin also saw what equipment Alfred used, how he prepared his coffee in the shop, and how he determined price. "He didn't say how we had to do it within our own company, but he made sure we found out for ourselves, with his help."

Of course, the three also learned how to "cup," or professionally taste coffee. Or rather, Alfred gave them the technique they needed to master it, because it would be impossible to learn all there is to know within the course of a single week. As Baldwin noted, "Alfred couldn't develop our taste, but he taught us what to look for in the coffee."

After their internships, they negotiated with Alfred to provide them with his beans. He might have thought the arrangement wouldn't last long, Bowker said. "I think he knew by then that we were going to roast our own beans and differentiate ourselves from Peet's."

WHAT'S IN THE FRENCH ROAST?

Alfred was willing to share his knowledge, but he could also be secretive about his contacts and especially his coffee blends, Baldwin remembered. "Zev was reprimanded once because he was looking into some papers of Alfred's. He was very reserved about giving out any information with regard to his blends." Baldwin experienced that himself when he asked Alfred directly what the composition of the French Roast was. "Alfred started a long story that didn't make me any wiser. I asked him whether it was a prerequisite for a good coffee entrepreneur to be skilled in saying nothing with many words. And he laughed."

However, Alfred was very forthcoming when it came to connecting the three men with his top vendors. Through these connections, they were able to get coffees that were hard to find, especially in North America. In a glass case in the original shop in Berkeley, there is a cashbook of Alfred's in which he kept the names of the vendors, deliveries, and the prices, with great precision.

The three fledgling entrepreneurs also experienced how Alfred was constantly explaining to his customers how they had to make coffee. That was one of the most important lessons they learned in Berkeley. Their mentor knew that coffee could be of the highest quality, but if customers didn't make it properly, it would reflect badly (and unfairly) on the product. Or worse, they might share that conclusion with others. Often, customers were lectured if Alfred sensed that they made the coffee in the wrong way. For the same reason, he hated the much-used percolator machine in which the coffee was constantly boiled, imparting a bitter and burnt taste.

"Alfred was always ready to go when someone came in and had the nerve to ask for a pound of Major Dickason's, ground for a percolator," Siegl said. "The customer would not be spared, even while other customers and staff were around. Alfred would say, 'I don't want you to use my coffee in a percolator. It's a bad method—the coffee will burn. Why don't you use a proper coffee maker or a filter system?' And his voice would increase in volume as he was saying this, so that everyone in the shop could hear it."

For his American customers—usually king and always right—Alfred's approach must have been shocking.

"First and foremost, he was a teacher. How he loved to explain things!" Siegl said. "I heard from people that he liked to lecture, but for me that isn't a negative quality if you truly are an expert. That was the case with Alfred. He had learned all of this throughout his life and hadn't picked it up from a book."

"Alfred was very formal but he was also very funny," Bowker recalled. "He was a complicated man, but he always treated me with respect and kindness. It was clear that I knew much less about coffee than he did, and I was much younger. But he was never pretentious or unkind. He was very self-assured about how things should be done and because we had respect for that, he respected us."

Baldwin felt that he got to know Alfred in that week as a "very intelligent person. He was charming, an expert, and he had a great interest in culture." In the years that followed, it was Baldwin who, of the three founders, had the most intense relationship with Alfred. "It became clear to me that even though Alfred was very successful, he was eager to be recognized. That never went away. All those conflicts with his father—he must have thought that he was never good enough."

STARTING OFF WITH A TIGHT BUDGET

After their return to Seattle, Baldwin, Bowker, and Siegl got to work on getting Starbucks up and running. Each of them invested $1,350 and added onto the starting capital with an extra $5,000 from a bank loan. It was a tight budget, so they made the store's shelves and sign themselves. To start a company in Seattle in the beginning of the seventies was a daring thing to do; the city was suffering from mass layoffs at Boeing, the largest employer in the Northwest at that time. There was a cynical billboard at Seattle's airport that read, WILL THE LAST PERSON LEAVING SEATTLE TURN OFF THE LIGHTS?

In March 1971, they opened their store and they were lucky that the *Seattle Times* came by and wrote a glowing review. Because of that, people began to drop in. At the beginning, only Siegl worked full-time for the company and had a salary. Serial entre-

NO STARBUCKS WITHOUT PEET'S

preneur Bowker could fall back on his income from his advertising and design agency, and Baldwin still made an income teaching composition and rhetoric. During lunch, the three would discuss their business.

As promised, Alfred delivered his beans to Starbucks. The three copied the mantra of their mentor: The quality of coffee could not be compromised by anything. But Alfred's influence reached further than that. You could tell by the way in which the store was designed. You could see it in the inclusion of spices (Starbucks – Coffee, Tea & Spices), the woodwork along the walls, the shape of the collection bins for the coffee, the small coffee bar for the tasting, and the emphasis on the sale of coffee beans for making coffee at home. It all went back to Alfred's ideas in Berkeley.

"We had copied Peet's. The whole place was modeled after what Alfred had done, and he had given us his permission to do so," Baldwin said.

Siegl added, "The shops we opened in Seattle in the seventies were heavily inspired by Alfred's ideas. For years, customers could sample the coffee so they could decide which beans to buy. For ten years, we used the same model he used."

THE FIRST STARBUCKS

The first Starbucks store, on 2000 Western Avenue, is no longer in existence. But for those who want to know what it looked like, they don't have to go far. In 1976, the entire shop was moved one block away to a new store on Pike Place, the famous market area of Seattle. Since then, this store has been known as the first Starbucks of Seattle, and it has become one of the more popular tourist attractions of the city. But visitors who think that it might be a replica of the Starbucks they know today, with couches and chairs, are in for a surprise. You can hardly sit anywhere, but there are plenty of different kinds of coffee beans to take home.

In a picture from 1971, you can see the three founders in their store. It seems as if they even copied Alfred's way of dressing: Shirt and tie, plus an apron (replacing the shopcoat old-fashioned grocers—and Alfred—used to wear). Baldwin clarified that they only dressed up for the picture. "In the store, we never wore a tie." The apron, however, had a staying power, even after Starbucks changed course and the bean sellers behind the counters were traded in for baristas behind espresso machines. Then it became the barista apron.

While the three felt that they had been "adopted" by Alfred, he kept the relationship professional, and sometimes he did so in bizarre ways.

"One day, I had forgotten to send a check for the coffee we had ordered," Baldwin said. "Alfred didn't call to ask where his check was; he simply stopped sending any more coffee. Truly bizarre. We had had a business relationship for quite a while, we always paid on time and because he had stopped sending coffee, we were suddenly short." No check: no coffee, seemed to be the message. There have been other loyal clients of Alfred's who went through the same experience.

At the same time, Alfred would visit his pupils in Seattle and check out their shop. He was probably quite content. After all, he looked at a replica of his own store. When Starbucks decided to open another store, a year after opening their first, Alfred decided that the time had come for Baldwin, Bowker, and Siegl to roast their own beans.

Baldwin remembers, "Alfred told us that we had gotten too big. 'I can't deal with the volume. You need your own roaster.' He found one for us in the Netherlands and negotiated the sale. He may have made some money off of it himself." The coffee roaster arrived in a container at Starbucks but it consisted of different parts that needed to be assembled. "It did come with some copied pages of a German manual, but, in the end, we did manage to put it together."

Baldwin then went down to Berkeley again for a week to learn more on how to roast. The different roles within Starbucks had become quite clear at that point: Baldwin was responsible for the coffee and daily management; Bowker, the creative power behind the company, was in charge of positioning and marketing; and Siegl led retail growth (along with business experiments such as coffee beans for supermarkets and the import of coffee grinders from Germany).

When they started roasting their own beans, Alfred's influence was still felt, Siegl said. "Companies asked us to roast their coffee beans and we tried it. But we decided against it almost immediately—we felt we were prostituting ourselves." The quality was simply not up to par. "Many coffee companies do it, as it's good for sales, but our decision not to do it was because of Alfred: We didn't want to compromise quality."

A FATHER FIGURE

The fact that Alfred came by several times indicated that he kept more than just an average interest in the company that had been inspired by him. He trusted the three young men as resellers of his coffee and that was quite something for Alfred, who always wanted to be in complete control as far as his coffee was concerned.

In their descriptions of their mentor, the three Starbucks founders referred to him as a father figure or uncle ("the one who teaches you a lesson"). "But we were prepared to learn. I think that's why he liked us. He never had a son and maybe he fostered that kind of connection with one of us, or even all three," Bowker explained. The reverse, he said, was certainly true, "I grew up without a father because he was killed in World War II. There were very few male role models in my life."

"It always seemed as if he was happy to see us, like an uncle who visited his successful nephews," Siegl remembered. "One day, I took him to a concert of chamber music at my parents' house. He was clearly having a good time. I was glad I could do something in return for everything he had given us."

Bowker, who had several companies besides Starbucks, showed Alfred his new brewery, Redhook Ale Brewery, one day. It was a so-called microbrewery, small in size to produce quality beer, and meant solely for the local market. "Alfred was fascinated by the small scale of the operation. He looked at me and said, 'I love small companies.'"

When, at the end of the eighties, Starbucks increased in size very quickly, under CEO Howard Schultz, Alfred became more critical. Because Starbucks developed in a way that he didn't approve of, he expressed some bitter feedback. Thus, in the documentary *Coffee Culture USA*, the eighty-seven-year-old Alfred denigrated the size of coffee drinks. In his view, they weren't in the coffee business; they were in the milk business. He didn't drop the name Starbucks, but it was clear to whom he was referring.

That said, in 2006, he also told the Dutch newspaper *NRC Handelsblad*, "Everything is about marketing and the anticipation of the changing demands of the customer, and Starbucks is terribly good at that." But it also came with a warning: "The bigger a company grows and the more products it offers, the higher the chance that the quality of the product declines." In spite of his critique of Starbucks, Alfred did continue to teach the roastmasters at the company in later years, both in Seattle and in Amsterdam, where Starbucks has an enormous coffee roasting plant. During those times, there was a mutual understanding, and only one person who was acknowledged as best.

FIRST REFUSAL

Baldwin always had a weakness for Peet's. Often, he had expressed that he wanted to be the first to hear if Alfred ever considered selling his company. In 1979, he received a call from Alfred about the acquisition of the company, but the message was not the one he had been hoping for: Alfred didn't offer his business for sale—he had already sold it.

"That was such a typical thing to do, without letting us know. I considered myself one of his sons. That he would do something like that, without even asking whether I'd be interested . . ." Even years after this incident, the memory of Alfred bypassing Baldwin seemed to trigger wistful disappointment when I was talking to him.

Nonetheless, a few years later, Baldwin would finally get his chance to buy Peet's.

"He blew the taste buds of the Folgers generation.
He created a coffee revolution from nothing."

—Laura Louis, Peet's bookkeeper, 1970s

6

A DIFFERENT OWNER

t the beginning of the seventies, Alfred Peet was unquestionably the most successful coffee entrepreneur on the West Coast. While the hippies were dwindling and vanishing from San Francisco and Berkeley, "Peetniks" showed up in the same numbers as they had since 1966. When Alfred opened his store in the mornings, lines of customers were waiting at the door, many with coffee mug in hand. For the rest of the day, this scene wouldn't change much.

Other coffee entrepreneurs were still making their pilgrimages to Berkeley, hoping to pick up on the magic and take it back to their own companies, just like the three founders of Starbucks had done. The Gourmet Ghetto around Peet's began to pick up steam, too, and drew in more and more people. The general desire and demand for good coffee also went up, as an increasing number of people began to raise their own standards.

From the beginning, the revenues for Peet's were impressive. Soon, Alfred had to develop a new coffee roasting facility in Emeryville, near Berkeley, for the simple reason that he couldn't keep up with demand by just roasting coffee in the Royal #5 at his store on Vine Street.

A journalist from the Dutch newspaper *NRC Handelsblad* visited Alfred in 2000, about three decades after he started his business, for an interview and noted the growth of revenue: "With a solemn sense of formality, bordering on emotion, he showed me a handwritten piece of paper on which the revenue figures were mentioned since 1966. One doesn't have to know a lot of math to draw an accompanying chart whose revenue curve went straight up."

People in the Bay Area assumed that such a successful business had made Alfred a rich man by the time the seventies rolled around. During her visit to San Francisco, people were telling Mariette Merle that she must be "very happy" to have an uncle like Alfred. "He must be a millionaire" was the word on the street.

But despite his business success, Alfred didn't seem to alter his lifestyle much. He owned a nice house, located on Keith Street in Berkeley, that was largely hidden but had a gorgeous view of the San Francisco Bay. "It was a beautiful house, rather modern, but it was also rather empty," Merle said. "I remember a great stereo system and an enormous wardrobe. If he liked a shirt, he bought ten at once, and they would be neatly deposited, still in plastic, in that wardrobe."

Alfred didn't seem to be baffled by the success of his coffee shop. He'd say, "You saw people think: What has he got that made him so successful?" For him there was no mystery: He knew his product inside out. "There's little you can learn on top of that, aside from growing coffee on a plantation. Also, it's a matter of working hard, working really hard." It was clear that the Dutchman had fully embraced the American work ethic: "If you're interested in something and you work hard, you'll get there."

But there was one more important and driving factor: His father. There was a score to be settled, even though Henri Peet had been dead for years. "One day," Alfred said, "I was in my coffee roasting place in Emeryville and I thought: 'You bastard. I outdid you.' At that point, my company was already bigger than his. Sadly, my father had already died at that stage, so there was no one who was going to congratulate me. And I wondered, why should I still fight him? At that point, I realized that I had been trying to level with him the entire time. I enjoyed it when I had made it, but there was no one to share it with. And that was kind of a shame."

The tone was one of bitterness and revenge, but also tragedy. He would have wanted to rub in his business success. It meant retribution both for his father's doubt in him and Alfred's cold-hearted childhood in Alkmaar. But part of him also seemed to have wanted to share his success with his father.

A SINGULAR MAN

In the middle of the seventies, Peet's had about fifteen employees. One of them was Laura Louis who was his bookkeeper but later became a writer of short fiction and a poet. She was working at Peet's when the pressure of work and success began to take its toll on Alfred. He wanted to keep total control and management of the company, but with the second store in Menlo Park, which was an hour's drive away from Berkeley, that became problematic.

"I never saw Mr. Peet as the 'God of coffee,' like the others. To me, he was very down to earth and real, a mortal with human foibles," she observed. "I knew people looked up to him tremendously because he blew open the taste buds of the Folgers generation. He created a coffee revolution from nothing."

Maybe she won Alfred's trust and respect exactly because of those two things, Louis remarked. She didn't come for the coffee and was not cowed by the founder of the company, and, possibly, this contributed to the bond she had with Alfred. "He trusted me with his money and, in time, with his deepest personal concerns." At that point, Alfred was already confiding in her about another painful family matter that didn't come to light until later. It was a matter that would consume Alfred as much as the relationship he had had with his late father.

Louis said that it wasn't easy to work with him. "Mr. Peet didn't feel obligated to be nice. He came to the United States with nothing. Everything he achieved was through hard work and a persistent attention to detail and excellence. His was an exacting standard to which he held everyone. It was my way or the highway." Time and again, people echoed that characterization when they tried to describe Alfred. "He had his own code of conduct and stuck by it throughout his life."

At the same time, Alfred cared deeply about the well-being of his employees, and he supported them—with both financial and moral support—when they went through difficult times. Louis experienced that herself when she needed a surgeon and he quickly called a friend. He also paid higher salaries than similar positions elsewhere in the Bay Area.

That said, Alfred often argued with the managers he hired for his shops. Quickly, one after another was fired because Alfred felt the work wasn't done properly. "I understand the impulse, as I have high standards myself in my work. He had the right to be demanding, but people struggled with what they felt was micromanaging. Tact was not his strong suit."

In this period, it was not uncommon for Alfred to loudly admonish his employees when they, in his opinion, didn't do it right. Such outbursts would lead to turmoil in the shop, and Louis was the one to smooth out the wrinkles. "He never directed his wrath at me, nor would I have put up with it if he had. I didn't provoke him. Rather, I seemed to have a calming effect on him."

In part, Alfred brought these problems upon himself. He might have been more tolerant if he had acknowledged that not everyone would have his attention for detail. He also could have known that not everyone would do the work the way he did, simply because he was much more knowledgeable about coffee and tea. Those were insights that came much later. At the same time, his incessant determination to maintain his own high standards, a regimen he forced on his employees as well, did turn Peet's into an excellent and successful business. But his perfectionism isolated Alfred more and more from his own surroundings, and, in the end, it became all-consuming.

In 1978, a third Peet's was opened, on Piedmont Avenue. It was nearer than the one in Menlo Park, which made it easier for Alfred to watch (read: control) how business was faring there. He loved to walk and would take lengthy treks at a swift pace. He had long legs, "like a bird," Louis told me. "Later I realized that those long walks probably were a form of meditation for him, a way to process his problems."

However, it soon became apparent that the founder of Peet's was burning out. He needed to confront it alone, so it seems. "He didn't talk of any enduring relationships. There was a woman he cared for deeply at one time, but the business took all his attention. Despite a certain awkwardness and nervousness around women, he loved women, loved being around them. He appreciated beauty. And women liked him as well."

All in all, the long contemplative walks didn't help anymore. Something had to change.

THE TIME HAD COME

"I was about to turn sixty, and if I didn't leave the company, it might have devoured me. You'd get a heart attack or you're going to get sloppier and then you start to complain because you're doing things against your will. So, what do you do? You get out."

Alfred later described the sale of his coffee business as if he had sold a mere house. "Now it's finished, and someone else can live in it. They can neglect or ruin it. That's their problem, not mine. When I left it, the house was in perfect condition."

In retrospect, Alfred's explanation sounds almost cold and calculating, hiding an ambivalence that would surface soon after he had sold his business. Because, contrary to the impression he tried to give, Alfred had a difficult time letting go of his business. Shortly after the sale of Peet's, he suffered a brief depression.

Sal Bonavita bought the iconic coffee business in 1979. At the sale, Alfred had negotiated that for a period of five years, he would stay on as a consultant of the company. As a consultant, he'd be involved with the quality consistency of the coffee and tea, which was the part of the business he was really passionate about anyway.

Bonavita first came into contact with Alfred through his import company for coffee makers, he told me in his hometown of Tiburon, California, in May 2014. It was a clear day, and across the bay we could see the San Francisco skyline. Tiburon exuded peace and calm, and Bonavita, the grandson of Italian immigrants, blended in perfectly with the atmosphere as we ambled along the waterfront, while he told his story in thoughtful and subdued tones.

At the end of the seventies, Bonavita, through his import company Coffee Imports International, sold specialty coffee and tea, Italian espresso machines, cups, and a host of other coffee-related accessories to coffee shops throughout the United States, as well as to the luxury department stores Bloomingdale's and Macy's. "At one point, my company had 3,000 customers," he told me with pride. Before that, he had sold a company that provided coffee and coffee makers to offices and businesses. Business was good.

At Macy's, there was also a demand for coffee beans; thus it was decided to start opening "specialty coffee shops" in department stores. Bonavita came to oversee it all. The idea of small stores within larger department stores is more conventional now, but at that time it was a new thing. Bonavita didn't sell very many beans this way, but the shops did boost the sale of coffee makers and accessory equipment.

"One day, I looked at my sales and I noticed that a place in Berkeley sold more coffee supplies than some of the department stores I was doing business with. I called up my sales manager and said to him: 'Next time I'm going with you to Peet's. I want to meet the founder.'"

Whether it is a coincidence or not, this story resembles that of Howard Schultz's, the later CEO of Starbucks. As a representative for a series of products, Schultz had noticed that coffee filters were enormously popular in a shop in Seattle, and just like Bonavita, he decided to go and take a look to find out why this was the case.

A CHARMING BUT STERN TEACHER

"Alfred Peet was a totally different animal," Bonavita said, after being asked for a first impression of the Dutchman. "Most people in the coffee business were rather intimidated by him at the time. But he could certainly be charming as well. The more I got to know him, the more I got to see a soft side, which he didn't show to many

1

1. Young Alfred Peet (in the middle) together with his family.

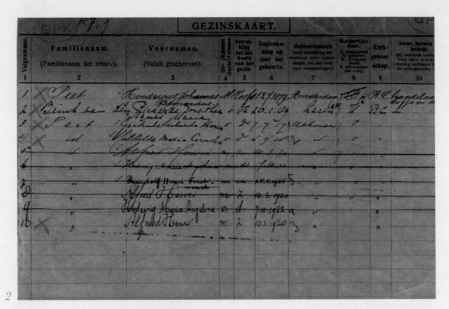

2. *Family administration at the archives in Alkmaar.*
3. *House where Alfred grew up in Alkmaar.*

4. *The two buildings to the right are Alfred's father's coffee business in Alkmaar.*

No. 8182920

Name PEET, Alfred Henry

residing at 2226 Divisadero St., San Francisco, Calif.

Date of birth MAR 10 1920 Date of order of admission SEP 8 1960

Date certificate issued SEP 8 1960 by the

U. S. District Court at San Francisco, California

Petition No. 143791 Alien Registration No. 8 922 243

M.E. (COMPLETE AND TRUE SIGNATURE OF HOLDER)

5

6

5. *Document for naturalization of Alfred to become a US citizen.*
6. *Place of Peet's in Berkeley early twentieth century.*

7

7. *Alfred at the roaster at his shop in Berkeley, in the late 1960s.*

8. *Three founders of Starbucks in their first shop in Seattle, 1971.*

9. *Alfred (standing right) with E.A. Johnson, early 1960s.*

10

10. *Alfred pouring beans in his shop.*

11

11. Alfred in his shop, late 1960s.

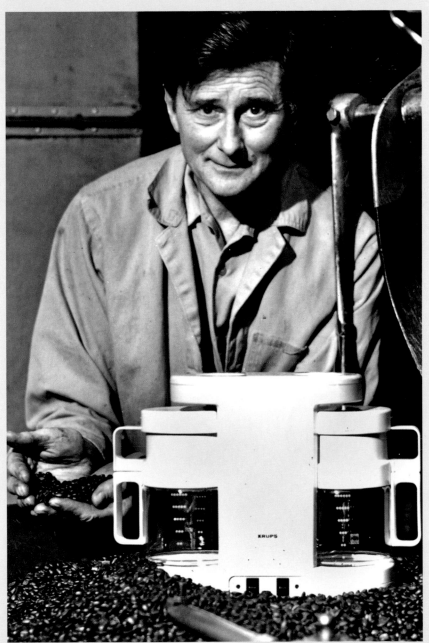

12

12. *Alfred, probably in Peet's roasting plant, mid-1970s.*

13. *Alfred in his shop, early 1970s.*
14. *Alfred and Jim Reynolds with employees from a Kenian coffee company, 1985.*

15. Poster made by Berkeley designer David Lance Goines for Peet's.

16. Fax from a customer, desperate for Peet's coffee, on display in the original Peet's in Berkeley.

17. First logo of Peet's in a 1960s style.

18

19

18.& 19. Customers in the first Peet's in Berkeley.

20

21

20. *The exterior of the first Peet's in Berkeley.*
21. *Redesigned Peet's on Chestnut Street, San Francisco.*

22. *The first roaster Alfred used at his shop in Berkeley, which was purchased by his pupil John Weaver and now resides at Weaver's Coffee.*

23. *Sal Bonavita and Alfred, early 1980s.*
24. *Jerry Baldwin, the cofounder of Starbucks, decided to buy Peet's in 1984.*
25. *Alfred, shortly before he died.*

people." But above all, Bonavita says, "he was a stern teacher, for everyone. It seemed like he was on a crusade in a quest for quality. That was the driving force: How do I improve quality?"

During their first meeting, Bonavita managed to draw Alfred's interest in his new coffee makers. "And he noticed my enthusiasm about roasting," Bonavita said. The plan for an acquisition developed gradually. Suddenly, it seemed a good business decision to buy Peet's as a supplier of coffee and as a retailer where Bonavita could sell his coffee makers. The deal appeared obvious.

At the time, Peet's was a "gold mine," Bonavita said. "It was all cash, I couldn't believe it." Bonavita, on the other hand, was used to sending invoices to his customers and then having to wait months to get paid. He had to fight to get his money, and sometimes he had to ask for credit from the bank to bridge the payment gap. "When I saw how things were done at Peet's, I was like, 'That's the way!'"

At first, Alfred ignored Bonavita's proposal, even though Bonavita had promised to respect the traditions of the company, like teaching customers about coffee and maintaining a devotion to quality. Several months went by, and then Alfred came with a counter proposal. "He said, 'I'm prepared to talk to you about a sale. But first you have to come here and taste coffee and tea with me so that I can determine whether you are capable enough to continue the business.' That was so typical of Alfred. He had to test you first." Bonavita had no choice but to become another of Alfred's students.

Jerry Baldwin of Starbucks and others had also expressed interest in acquiring the stores, but Alfred commented later that he had intentionally picked a "blank slate" to sell his company to.

He also added the requirement that the candidate had to first taste coffee and tea with him for weeks on end. "If I go for someone who thinks that they know everything about coffee and tea, then it's hard to change that. I said, 'Whether you have a penny or a million dollars in your pocket, you cannot buy this company if I don't have the feeling that I can make something out of you as a coffee entre-preneur. If I can't, the deal is off.' You've got to be very motivated if you want to take over this business. That was my message."

Because of Bonavita's plan to sell Peet's coffee in department stores and supermarkets, the negotiations were very cumbersome. Alfred didn't have any faith in that; he feared it would fail and that Peet's would change as soon as it started distributing its coffee else-where or being offered on the mass market. However, Alfred was in a strong negotiating position. He didn't have to sell the business because he needed the money, while Bonavita didn't have adequate resources to acquire the business. Because of that, Alfred essentially financed the acquisition by agreeing to a sum that was to be paid off over five years. After that, the business would be Bonavita's.

Bonavita didn't get all that he wanted due to Alfred's reserva-tions and conditions, but Bonavita had become so thrilled with the market for specialty coffee that he decided to go ahead with the deal anyway. "It was part of my original plan to also sell to depart-ment stores, but the deal was still worth it, and I knew I could wait until Alfred was paid off to expand the sale of Peet's coffee to other markets." In the meantime, he had become very involved in the movement of specialty coffee and he traveled all over the United States to give presentations on coffee and coffee making.

As mentioned, the negotiations were difficult at first. Alfred had hired one of the best law offices in San Francisco and was accompanied by five lawyers while Bonavita only had one. "After seven days, we had a meeting and I said to Alfred, 'At this rate, it'll cost almost $1,300 per hour to strike a deal. Can't we discuss it among ourselves during a weekend and save all that money?' The lawyers started protesting loudly, but we did it anyway." The next weekend, Alfred and Bonavita went to Napa Valley, the wine region north of San Francisco, to hike. "We got to know each other better and came to a deal."

At the time of the acquisition, Peet's consisted of two shops. A conflict related to the franchise establishment on Piedmont Avenue meant that Alfred had gotten rid of that particular store. Bonavita didn't want to divulge what he had paid for the two shops, but in light of a later deal, it must have been in the $1 to $2 million range, and likely closer to $2 million. Today, that amount would equal something like $6.5 million. For a coffee concern with only two shops that is quite a hefty amount, even now.

ALFRED'S DOUBTS

On occasion, Alfred appeared to have doubts about selling his business. He told Bonavita that he felt as if he had lost a child, and that he couldn't distance himself from it. Bonavita asked him repeatedly why he had sold the company if he still felt so involved. "He told me it had gotten out of hand and that he didn't have a life anymore. My decisions were disorienting to him because the company still felt like it was his own child. 'I saw it grow up,' Alfred said to me, a remark that showed he was still rather emotionally attached to the company."

Other entrepreneurs might decide to keep their company if they felt the same way; they might just hand over the daily management to someone else. Bonavita said, "For Alfred, that wasn't an option at all. Not a single manager would ever meet his expectations—every candidate was doomed to fail in advance. He was skeptical to hand over the reins if there was no one good or trustworthy enough to do it."

But later in life, there were also moments of introspection. In his conversation with the *East Bay Express*, Alfred indicated that it's natural to seek in others the same standards that you've set for yourself. But he added, "I think I expected too much. I didn't have the ability to get the best out of people." He also said, "I'm more an entrepreneurial type than a managerial type." At the same time, he noted that he had had a lot on his plate—import, production, wholesale, the shops—and that there was no time to be a "babysitter" and an "instructor."

In 2001, the business publication *Inc.* did a story on Alfred in their feature "My Biggest Mistake." The then-retired coffee pioneer admitted that he hadn't been good in personal relationships, and that he still would have been in business if he had had better people skills. He explicitly mentioned his inability to delegate. "I worked too hard because I couldn't delegate. I wanted to oversee everything. I said, 'I know exactly where I want to go, but I can't explain every thought, every idea I have for the future of this company.' Many people left. I was burnt out, so I had to sell. Do you know what it's like when you've given so much, there's nothing left? I sold my company and it broke my heart. Coffee was my life. But I'm over it now."

A month after he had sold the company, Alfred fired an employee, even though he wasn't authorized to do so. "His firing of that employee was rather rough," Bonavita said. "I had to point out to him that the colonial period was over and that you couldn't treat people that way." Despite Alfred's (false) assumption that he had successfully distanced himself from his company, and that it was up to others to be responsible for the business, in reality, nothing seemed to have really changed. Or rather: There were now two captains on the ship.

ALFRED WENT TOO FAR

During the negotiations, Alfred had been nothing but friendly to Bonavita. He dined with Bonavita and his wife and played with their children. But once the deal was done, that immediately changed. Alfred wondered what the new owner would do with his other "ridiculous" company as he felt that Bonavita would have to dedicate himself fully to Peet's. Tempers ran high when Alfred, during Bonavita's absence, bought a large batch of coffee without informing Bonavita's brother-in-law who managed the business on his behalf.

"I returned from a trade show in Milan, and Alfred said, 'I sold my business to you, not to your brother-in-law.' And then he mentioned that he had bought some coffee for $300,000. I was stunned. 'How can you force me to commit to such an amount? Where am I supposed to get the money from?' I replied. 'You're not the owner of this company. I am. Understood?'"

Alfred answered that this is how he had done business all his life. It was the only way to get consistent quality, he explained to Bonavita, and it would be better than having to buy coffee every month. But Alfred realized he had gone too far and the day after that, he returned to do some damage control.

"I was still irritated and angry," Bonavita remembered. "He opened with a story about a friend of his who was willing to

finance the purchase. It's possible that he was that friend himself."
Of course, there was one precondition to this solution. For three
months, Bonavita had to come to the coffee roasting facility to roast
coffee and really learn the trade. After three months, the relationship
improved, Bonavita said, and, in its place emerged a friendship.

It was the second time that Alfred had forced the owner to
become his student. It had also been a precondition to the sale, for
Bonavita was only eligible to buy the company if he would roast
coffee daily with the founder. He could have gotten out of that if
he had taken over the company by paying the total sale price. But
the roasting wasn't an unwelcome compulsory chore—Bonavita
admitted he also enjoyed that period. "With an eye for detail,
Alfred set everything on the table in preparation, which meant ten
to fifteen cups. Then he weighed and ground the coffee. When we
had tasted everything, he tidied up. In his willingness to reverse our
roles, I saw Alfred's tender side. These were the most pleasurable
moments we had together."

When Bonavita was preparing for a tea tasting, Alfred inter-
rupted him once. Bonavita said, "He threw his hands up in the air
and yelled, 'The guy doesn't even know how to boil water!' It was
an important lesson. Alfred was hyper-focused on all the processes
around making tea, which meant that not only the water—soft,
hard, containing minerals, chlorinated—had to be prejudged, but
the same applied to the temperature of the water. Since then, I feel
that even boiling water is not a straightforward thing."

When customers asked questions about coffee, Alfred would
still get excited. "At those moments, it was like he was on a stage
and gave a performance. And it wasn't just talk; he'd let people
smell coffee and asked them what they thought. Alfred mesmerized

people," Bonavita explained. "Once my wife said when we were tasting tea again, and we exchanged some precise words of appreciation about flavors, 'If I weren't here,' she said, 'I'd be thinking you two were discussing women.'"

Bonavita is not surprised by the tremendous impact Alfred has had as a coffee entrepreneur. For the first time, a broad audience was educated about coffee: "For most people it was a totally new thing; coffee came from cans from General Foods, Folgers, and the other big mass producers of coffee. But with his enthusiasm and knowledge, he elevated you to a level which was completely outside of your own realm of experience."

OPENING NEW STORES

In the first year after he bought Peet's, Bonavita opened another store. He wanted to add a store every year, which was something Alfred didn't like at all but which he became resigned to in the end. The revenue per square foot in the stores "was astounding," Bonavita said. The revenues of his other company were higher, but the profitability of Peet's was much better. This was clear from the sheer number of customers who kept coming back: Every morning Bonavita had to push through a crowd of waiting customers to enter the shop.

"Alfred didn't see the need to grow any further," Bonavita told me. "It was almost like a Japanese Zen kind of thing; the notion that you only do that which you can do perfectly. To aim for perfection was more important to him than making money."

Bonavita also expanded the business via mail. From the beginning, there was a demand from other parts of the country, which was initially triggered by students and professors who had studied and worked at UC Berkeley, and who, after leaving the university, missed their daily cup at Peet's. Bonavita saw this sale via mail as a separate store. "It was part of a humongous potential." There is still a fax in existence from a later time (kept in the little museum area at the first Peet's) in which a desperate customer says it all: "Send coffee. Fast please!"

The difference in vision between the two men as to how the coffee business ought to be run became clearer over time. One day, the coffee roaster broke down and Bonavita had to help fix it. "For Alfred, it was a beautiful moment. We had to disassemble the entire machine and he wanted to teach me about every single part." Bonavita was used to having a manager and multiple staff members who all had different tasks. "In my view, the person who roasted the coffee was a different person from the one who sold it to customers. Alfred felt that you had to know everything about coffee beans, as well as run every aspect of the business."

There was still another difference in management styles, and that amounted to frugality, which may be seen as a typically Dutch trait. The backs of envelopes and letters were used to write on. No coffee bean was lost. Alfred swept them from the floor and threw them back into the roaster with the excuse that any dust it had picked up would get burned off in the process anyway. At home, he showed a similar thriftiness, even though the former entrepreneur had become a wealthy man due to his business. "When I started working with him, I noticed that he wasn't much different at home. He used a tea crate as a table. The guy had enough money to buy a decent table, but he was watching every penny."

But money wasn't the overriding concern when Alfred saw that people couldn't take care of themselves anymore. When he walked past a center for handicapped elderly in San Francisco one day, he took a peek inside and heard there were funding problems. A day later, the center received a check for $20,000. He also gave money to cultural institutions and was on the board of a number of charities. Those in his immediate environment weren't aware of that part of Alfred's life. It was only after his death that people discovered the full scope of his philanthropic activities.

"Deep inside him there was a beautiful soul. Sometimes you'd see a glimpse of it," Bonavita said. "However, the overwhelming image I have of him is that of a tormented man. It always went back to his father. 'The guy was impossible,' he'd say. More than once he'd tell me he wished he'd had an Italian father. The Dutch mother was fine, but an Italian father was what he wished for."

"Alfred was my first mentor," Bonavita continued, alluding to the fact that his own father had been away from home a lot due to his work. "Alfred taught me a profession for the rest of my life."

THE ONE AND ONLY COFFEE ROASTER

"This is it. This is what started the coffee revolution," John Weaver said while we were in San Rafael, north of San Francisco. "This is the coffee roaster that Alfred Peet used in Berkeley." The most remarkable parts are the form of the cylinder and the shiny brass—these days, coffee roasters are predominantly black.

Weaver showed a sense of pride. The coffee roaster can be found at the entrance of his coffee business, and every day when he comes in, it reminds him of the period when he worked together with Sal Bonavita and Alfred Peet in the early eighties. With his pointy beard, reflective sunglasses, and cap, Weaver looked more like a rock musician than a roastmaster. Young at heart, he still rides a surfboard on a regular basis. "Maybe I'll go out for a bit later on," he said when our conversation was ending. Weaver laughed a lot, especially when he was reminded of a funny incident, and then he'd say: "Ah, I have another great story for you . . ."

In almost everything, Weaver seemed the polar opposite of his teacher Alfred. Initially, Alfred wondered what to do with the young man who had come to the company as a delivery driver. But Alfred molded Weaver into the kind of roastmaster he wanted him to be. The espresso that Weaver offered me during the interview was of the kind that stays with you—and that is telling in itself, especially once one has become aware of the great quality and range of coffee you can now get in San Francisco. On the wall, close to the legendary coffee roaster, there was a recommendation letter from Alfred, which was written when Weaver was thinking of leaving Peet's in the early '90s. Alfred called him "a roastmaster with an excellent ability to taste coffee." He also recommended him as someone who maintained "the highest standards for coffee roasting."

"I really wanted to paint," Weaver said. "That's how I ended up loving to roast coffee, because it involves creativity, too. Roasting coffee is the art of creating flavor."

When Weaver approached Peet's for a job in 1980, he talked to both Bonavita and Alfred at the coffee roasting facility of Peet's in Emeryville. "There was something romantic about it, the whole place, with that coffee roaster. It was somewhat dark and felt mysterious, almost medieval."

At the time, Weaver worked in the meat processing industry, and in Emeryville he discovered a completely different world that appealed to him instantly. He wanted to work at Peet's so badly that he came back three times to ask about the job. He had no idea that Peet's had become such an institution—he only learned of that once he broke the news at home that he was going to be working there. "My parents told me that Peet's was the best coffee in the world."

Immediately after he got the job, Weaver had been warned about Alfred. Don't try to lie to him, he had heard from one colleague. The day prior, Alfred had fired Weaver's predecessor because he had lied about something as mundane as emptying a vacuum cleaner. Once he started working for Peet's, Weaver was in awe: He saw how Alfred passed newly roasted and very hot coffee beans through his hands. "Why would you do that, I asked myself, but maybe he did it to show that he was a tough guy who could simply do that."

Weaver went on, "Alfred was very strict and disciplined but he also had a very wry sense of humor. He was totally dismissive of the feelings or opinions of others. He only wanted things to be done the way he wanted them done." It seems somewhat puzzling that Weaver, who described himself as more relaxed, could work with someone like Alfred. Looking back, Weaver explained that it was "just really refreshing for me. He reminded me of my Czechoslovakian mother."

Weaver learned how to taste coffee and learned Alfred's methods. At one of the first sessions, there were three tables with about twenty coffees. Alfred was watching and after all the tasting was done, he asked Weaver which one was his favorite. The coffee novice quickly made his choice. His preference went to the Kenyan, as it was less complex than the other ones. "Alfred said, 'You're wrong.' I was completely taken aback. How could I be wrong about my favorite? But he said, 'The Guatemalan is your favorite, or it will be your favorite in the end.' And he was right; now Guatemalan coffees are my favorites because of their complexity.

"One morning about three weeks after I started my roasting training, I was roasting on the big roaster. I had just made a cup of coffee and was pouring a small amount of cream into it when Alfred surprised me coming around the corner. Instantly, he slapped the cup out of my hand and exclaimed, 'You will never put milk in my coffee! You will never learn to taste or roast coffee if you do!' The full cup of coffee had landed right in the trash can next to the roaster. To this day I never put anything in my coffee."

Weaver wouldn't be the first or last one who'd be thrown off by Alfred's way of teaching. The Dutchman tried to teach his students (and customers) that they had to develop their taste. His message was that initially you may like a coffee, but once you develop your taste, you learn to recognize and appreciate better coffees.

Alfred also showed his student how he worked the coffee roaster, including the mechanics. One day, one of the coffee roasters made a funny sound, and Weaver thought it was a quick fix but was proven wrong. "It took me two weeks. Two weeks! After that, I ran into the office to tell Sal and Alfred I had fixed it. From his face, I could tell that Alfred knew all along what had been the problem. This upset me slightly, but he just wanted me to experience finding the solution for myself. I assume the whole two weeks he sat there in his office and giggled about it."

CONFLICTS AND RESPECT

But the twenty-year-old Weaver also clashed often with Alfred. Where others might sigh or shake their heads when remembering their differences of opinion with Alfred, Weaver just had to laugh when he recalled his days with the coffee master.

For instance, there was the time when Weaver suggested they sell their beans in supermarkets. He didn't know then that Alfred had specifically negotiated that the coffee wouldn't be sold in supermarkets. Weaver pitched the idea to Alfred and Bonavita. "I told them they were ignoring an enormous market, and I suggested I'd cut off my long hair, put on a suit and try to sell it to those supermarkets. Alfred and Sal listened but then Alfred said with an angry expression on his face, 'Go back out there and roast the coffee.' As I left and closed the door, I heard him say, 'See, I warned you about this.'"

But there were also moments when Alfred wasn't on top of things. That happened when Jamaican Blue Mountain, one of the most expensive coffees in the world, had to be roasted. "Three times it failed when Alfred was doing it: The beans came out too dark. Sal became more and more anxious and said at one point, 'You roast the batch.' I was really scared but it became one of the best-roasted coffees that I can remember. Alfred had to laugh about the whole thing."

And then there was Weaver's accident with a forklift when a pallet shattered and about three-thousand pounds of Costa Rica coffee beans came crashing down. Alfred scolded Weaver, "You're gonna kill somebody!" But Weaver lashed out. "I got off the lift, pointed at it and said, 'You get on that thing and drive it!' It became awfully silent then. The truck driver Clyde then said with a deep voice, 'Oh boy, Weaver, you're gonna get it now.' But Alfred got this wan smile on his face as if he were thinking, 'Finally, that kid dares to stand his ground.' He turned around and walked away into the office, without saying anything. For the rest of the day he remained silent towards me, but slightly smiling all the time."

One day, when they opened a crate with tea from Germany, the two discovered a hidden compartment within the crate. Alfred told his younger colleague that it was used for smuggling opium. "He told me that on one of his travels through China he had smoked opium but that he hadn't liked the deep slumber that came over him." He also warned Weaver about the use of cocaine. "Alfred insisted I never use it because it would destroy my sense of taste."

Next, Weaver started telling me about the coffee roaster at the entrance of his business, Weaver's Coffee & Tea. "I still remember looking curiously at the Royal upstairs at Peet's, just two years after I started working there. Alfred came in, and he said, 'One day you should buy that one from Sal and start your own coffee business.' At the time, I thought he was crazy . . ."

Then the story of how it ended up at his company unfolded. "One evening I was driving home from surfing, and I was called by an old colleague from Peet's in San Rafael, California, who had gotten the roaster from Sal. He wanted to sell it and asked what it would be worth." Weaver became very excited and drove directly to where his friend was keeping it. They agreed on a price. But later that evening the seller had second thoughts. "He thought he might fetch $30,000, so he offered it to Peet's in an email. I pulled my offer, I didn't want to bid against my old employer. Peet's never responded, they were pinching pennies as they had just built a new roasting facility." So, Weaver waited. Three months went by, and then there was a phone call. A day later, he drove his truck to San Rafael.

After he came home, Weaver called Alfred immediately and told him about the purchase. "Alfred couldn't believe it. He almost fainted when he heard I had paid $10,000 for it." According to Weaver, Alfred told him to keep the roaster in his family if he could, in case Peet's came looking for it.

Eventually, the roaster "will go to the Smithsonian," Weaver said. "It's the coffee roaster that started everything here in the United States, but possibly the rest of the world as well."

ANGER ABOUT THE SALE

In 1984, something happened that Alfred had feared all along. Peet's founder flew off the handle when he heard that Bonavita had plans to sell the business. John Weaver remembered, "He stormed in, cursed as if he were possessed and yelled, 'I knew it. For Sal, it was nothing more than a real estate deal!'"

He seemed disillusioned that the company had ended up with someone who would resell with a profit after only a couple of years, just as one does in the real estate world. He had tried everything to hand it over as if it were a family company, which included considerable training and an emphasis upon the traditions that had to be respected.

Weaver himself was also upset when he heard about the sale, "I broke down in tears. I just couldn't believe it."

But Bonavita had his reasons to sell. His wife had become seriously ill, and he felt there was no option but to get rid of the company and focus on his family. In Tiburon, Bonavita talked about his family situation and how, for years, they had been searching for special treatments, from Mexico to Tibet. But he wanted to keep it private. "There were bigger responsibilities at that moment, and the sale was for me a way to deal with that," he told me. "It was very painful; I was attached to Peet's. But at the time, it was the right decision and looking back, I never regretted it."

At first, Bonavita tried to appoint Alfred to be responsible for the company in his absence but the founder declined. To his amazement, Alfred told him, "Keep the company and deal with it." Alfred was frequently at Peet's and was involved with everything, so how much trouble would it have been for him to oversee the business in the meantime? But Alfred didn't want to hear about it, and from the fear on his face, Bonavita saw that the founder didn't want to return to those last years when he had been managing Peet's, a period that had almost triggered a personal burn-out. "He had no family life and he didn't understand that you'd make such a family decision," Bonavita commented. "He didn't see that family could be more important than business."

Over the years, there had been several parties that had shown an interest in acquiring Peet's. According to Bonavita, he might have gotten a better price from a sale to Hills Bros. or one of the other big coffee companies, but instead he called Jerry Baldwin. Just as the Starbucks cofounder had asked Alfred to call him in the event of a possible sale, so had he asked Bonavita to call him first if he ever thought of selling Peet's. "Without a doubt, Jerry was the best person to continue Peet's," Bonavita said.

Slowly but surely, Alfred's anger over the sale quieted down. A few years after that, contact between Alfred and Sal was renewed when Bonavita called him out of the blue. "I guess we went out to taste some coffee." Bonavita asked him then whether his former teacher had forgiven him. He had, and Alfred added, "I understand it."

After that, the two started seeing each other regularly again. They would hike around San Francisco, and they met up at the new coffee shop Bonavita had started in Mill Valley in 1990, near San Francisco. In a picture dating back to that time, the two are seen together again, smiling generously and—as ever—tasting coffee.

"That's how people viewed him, like the God of coffee."

—Jim Reynolds, Starbucks roastmaster

7

TWO COMPANIES

 t was my lucky day," Starbucks cofounder Jerry Baldwin said, when he heard that he could buy Peet's. In 1984, thirteen years after the founding of Starbucks, he was offered the opportunity that he had previously missed out on. He was given the news during a lunch with Sal Bonavita and tried to hide his excitement by going to the bathroom.

Back then, Starbucks and Peet's were comparable companies: They sold coffee beans predominantly, as well as coffee makers and other coffee-related accessories, and they only had a few shops. In Seattle, there were five locations for Starbucks and the Bay Area had four locations for Peet's.

Another cofounder of Starbucks, Zev Siegl, had left the company already when the negotiations for an acquisition began. Later he'd admit that he felt more at ease in a start-up. Starbucks, in the meantime, had become more of an established company where the pioneering of the three founders had made room for the managing of a larger company with dozens of people.

At the time of the acquisition, Howard Schultz, the future CEO of Starbucks, was working on his dream of an espresso bar. In a new Starbucks shop in Seattle, he was given the opportunity in 1984 to experiment with the serving of espressos and cappuccinos, which he had come to love during a trip to Italy. "We were all enthusiastic about serving coffee in the stores in the future,"

Baldwin says. "All of us liked the energy that was generated by people drinking coffee in the store." He says Schultz and Bowker, "who had become enamored of espresso during a trip in 1963 to Italy," set out to develop the idea of the espresso bar, and he himself supervised the design and construction of the store. It became the sixth store of Starbucks. Before Starbucks had served coffee, just like Alfred had done, to give people the chance to taste the coffee.

Soon, cappuccinos and lattes became a popular addition to the Starbucks menu. According to Schultz, he was the one who introduced the latte to the United States—a combination of espresso with milk, which he supposedly discovered in Verona, Italy. That statement may have to be taken with a grain of salt. It's highly likely that the latte was already served in Italian-American restaurants and cafés, and people have pointed out that Café Allegro in Seattle, the business of Dave Olsen, was a precursor to coffee drinks, based on espresso. Nonetheless, at Starbucks, Schultz turned "latte" into a household name for coffee drinkers in the United States.

BORROWING MONEY

When Starbucks and Peet's had the same owners (they kept their independence as separate stores), Ronald Reagan was president and the American economy grew by leaps and bounds. Alfred would show his admiration for the Republican president, although he did this partially to provoke his liberal friends in Berkeley. Banks and other financial lenders were eager to advance money to companies with acquisition plans in the Reagan era. In hindsight, those loans happened all too easily, which resulted in many

American banks and institutions going under in the second half of the eighties.

At the time of the deal, Starbucks was still riding the wave of the favorable economic tide. "We paid $4 million for Peet's," Baldwin said. "And that was an enormous amount of money at the time. But banks were more than happy to lend money. The acquisition we brought about could never be repeated today."

The acquisition of Peet's, for which Baldwin and Bowker also got help from friends, resulted in deep debts for Starbucks. According to Baldwin, for every dollar the shareholders had invested in Starbucks, the company owed thirteen dollars to the bank.

The acquisition sum for Peet's was high. Baldwin doubted whether he could pay the amount that Bonavita had in mind: "It wasn't realistic." But Bonavita's attorney found a workaround. He quickly noticed how eager the "Peetniks" from Seattle were, and recognized it as a point of leverage for the sellers. Baldwin said that he wasn't very experienced in business at that point, and that he wasn't advised properly at the time of the purchase.

Their "solution" was this: The price could be inflated by resorting to certain tax rules that Bonavita's attorney suggested. Under these rules, possessions of the company for sale (Peet's) could be added when determining the collateral for the bank, and thus it became possible to borrow a higher sum from the bank.

Baldwin couldn't stand Bonavita's attorney. "You couldn't have a normal conversation with him without being challenged and hear that you were being an idiot. He was much more aggressive than the attorney who accompanied me. At one point,

I said, 'Sal, if he comes with you at the signing, I won't sign.' It wasn't my style to say it that way, but I felt very strongly about it at the time."

That said, Baldwin never had any buyer's remorse. "Never. Not for a moment. That's for sure."

ALFRED AS A CONSULTANT

When the acquisition of Peet's was concluded, Jim Reynolds, the roastmaster who worked for Starbucks, contacted Alfred. The Peet's founder was about to retire, but he was talked into returning to Peet's for one year. On a weekly basis, Alfred and Reynolds discussed the state of affairs and the quality of coffee. They'd taste together, too, which was the best way to learn about coffee. Baldwin would join them often as well. He could have learned one thing from Bonavita: Taking in Alfred meant that Baldwin would be "offered" more than just nonbinding advice.

Reynolds tried to benefit as much as he could from the presence of the famous coffee master. Reynolds had joined Starbucks years ago through a job ad. That the job involved coffee roasting was not included in the ad, and he was startled to find himself opposite the coffee roaster one day. Without any experience but with a little guidance from Baldwin, the novice tried to make it work. "In the beginning, I could brown the beans, but that was about it." From Alfred he learned "important aspects such as the modification of the temperature during the roasting." But Alfred also taught him to compare coffees, develop better tasting skills, and the importance of staying focused while working with coffee.

"It wasn't easy to work with him," Reynolds said. I met the amiable roastmaster at his house in Berkeley where he still follows the trends and developments in the coffee world from a distance. "If you didn't adopt his standards or follow his way of working, he'd get angry. And often he'd dump on me." At the same time, he heard from others that Alfred was fond of him. "I remember thinking, jeez, if this is how you get treated when he likes you, what would he do if he didn't like you?" Reynolds said, while laughing.

He still remembered seeing Alfred walk into Starbucks in 1974. It was his first meeting with the Dutchman. Alfred never announced his arrival in Seattle. He would simply turn up. "This caused a notable amount of stress. There was a feeling that God had just entered the building. That's how people viewed him, like the God of coffee. You never knew how he was going to react and that made me nervous."

After observing Reynolds at Starbucks that year, Alfred came to Baldwin, and told him that for Reynolds, "the coffee lives." It was a very high compliment.

In that first period after the acquisition, Alfred remained an important source of knowledge for the owners. He could indicate exactly what elements were important in coffee, Reynolds told me, but he also knew how to communicate what the customer expected of Peet's. Baldwin disclosed that Alfred's contribution at that time was more than welcome. Starbucks was doing well "but we didn't have the depth of knowledge and the experience that Alfred had."

"I loved how he exuded his European roots," Reynolds said. "The coffee world is a very old one, and in him you saw the connection with the past."

In 1985, Reynolds traveled to Kenya with Alfred. "Actually, he thought it rather strange to travel to coffee-producing countries. Now it's very common for coffee entrepreneurs to do that, but he had hardly done it at all. Others didn't do it either in those days." In Kenya, the two really got to know each other better.

The trip to Kenya was captured wonderfully in a picture in which Reynolds and Alfred are seen tasting coffee with two employees of the local company. In front of them there is a table with a few cups, and behind them there is a wall with shelves and cans with coffee. Alfred's dress code seemed to have caught on. While the two Kenyans wear shirts with ties and even a shopcoat, Alfred just wears a short-sleeved shirt. When you look at the picture, your eye is immediately drawn to Alfred's focus: His commanding presence clearly conveys that the ultimate judgment is his to make.

EXPANSION OF PEET'S

As soon as he was in charge of both Starbucks and Peet's, Baldwin began with the expansion of Peet's. Alfred was skeptical of expansion when the company was in Bonavita's hands. He hadn't changed his mind about it. He felt that expansion was a moot point because the current stores generated a lot of income. Or rather, that's what other people speculated. Alfred himself didn't make many public statements about the period in which Starbucks and Peet's were in the same hands, nor would he say anything about other developments vis-à-vis his former company in the eighties. "Clearly, Jerry had other ideas about how the company had to grow and be financed," Reynolds summarized. Obviously, the gap between the master and his pupil was becoming more pronounced.

Peet's and Starbucks had different company cultures. In Seattle, Starbucks was seen as a cult brand with an elitist touch. Reynolds explained, "People said we made coffee for fancy people." Peet's image, on the other hand, was very different when he and Baldwin started leading the company. "People were in love with Peet's. Even though Alfred had alienated some of his customers because of his behavior, the company was immensely popular. It was fantastic to be a part of that."

Meanwhile, at Peet's there was a genuine fear that Starbucks would start to dominate and that Peet's would lose its character because of it. Baldwin, who was from the Bay Area himself, knew that they'd be watched closely: "Seattle was very quiet, almost like a backwater, so we were free to do with Starbucks whatever we wanted to do, without receiving the criticism that we would have received in the Bay Area and elsewhere."

Just as Alfred was accustomed to walking into Starbucks unannounced, so would he turn up at the coffee roasting facility of Peet's in Emeryville. He was the owner of the building, so he had the key. "Everyone was walking on eggshells," Reynolds remembered, but by now he knew how to deal with Alfred. If necessary, he would cut him off whenever he butted-in by dropping by unexpectedly or joining a meeting to which he hadn't been invited.

A year after the acquisition of Peet's, the contract with Alfred came to an end. For the first time, he distanced himself from the coffee business that he had founded. Reynolds didn't see Alfred for a number of years, but Baldwin talked to him regularly.

As for the original store in Berkeley, Alfred did stop by there, since he lived close by, in the hidden house on Keith Street. All he needed was one question and Alfred would return to his former role of teacher and connoisseur, telling anyone who wanted to listen about the coffee and tea at the store.

AN UNUSUAL BUSINESS DECISION

Two years after the acquisition, Gordon Bowker felt like taking a step back. "I was being overwhelmed by the things that were happening," he said. His ad agency was growing fast, he had helped a friend in Seattle with the starting of a newspaper, and he was also working on his start-up, Red Hook Ale Brewery. To top it off, he was about to get married and become a father. "I realized there were boundaries to what I could do. I've always had a lot of energy, but now I was getting worn out."

Bowker wanted to distance himself from Starbucks and, together with Baldwin, he looked for a way to sell his share of the company. The move that Baldwin made after that surprised many: He, too, sold his share, to continue with Peet's.

"Yes, it's a bit odd, isn't it?" Baldwin admitted, laughing apologetically. Odd is an understatement. What entrepreneur sells his own company to continue with another company in the same market (even though he was a co-owner of that company)? For $3.8 million, Starbucks ended up in the hands of Howard Schultz and a group of investors. This included all coffee matters great and small as well as the brand, but not the business division of Starbucks, which was named Caravali Coffees. That division had been sold just a few months earlier to a Seattle consortium headed by Bart Wilson.

That Baldwin had had a weakness for Peet's had been clear from the beginning. He felt that the company of his mentor embodied the soul of coffee. "Jerry had always been in love with Peet's. He wanted to have the company to continue both the tradition of Peet's and Starbucks," Bowker explained.

Baldwin himself had several business and personal reasons to choose Peet's. "I saw a lot of opportunity for growth," he said. Also, the return to the San Francisco Bay Area was a welcome change of scenery for him and his wife. "When the question arose as to which company to pick, my wife didn't hesitate for a moment, even though her hometown was Seattle. She often says it was her idea to keep Peet's."

Bowker, on the other hand, always thought it was a strange choice. But he was glad that there were no emotional obstacles for Baldwin to sell Starbucks. "All of it led to the fact that I had reached my goal and could simplify my life."

The burden of debt surrounding Starbucks/Peet's was not the reason for the sale, as there was no financial urgency or necessity to sell Starbucks. While there had been financial problems when they bought out Siegl (and Starbucks did have some cash-flow problems at the time of the acquisition), Bowker noted that "all of that had been resolved when Starbucks was sold. We sold the company for different reasons."

Could Baldwin have retained the entirety of both of Starbucks and Peet's? To buy out Bowker and continue with both companies, he would have had to get a loan with a bank, and that wasn't as easy as it had been a few years earlier. He could have looked for other investors but that would have also meant losing more control of the company.

The millions that came out of the sale gave Baldwin the leverage to buy out Bowker and to start with the execution of his expansion plans for Peet's. They built a new coffee roasting plant to replace the old one in Emeryville, and in 1987 Peet's opened two new stores.

"I still count myself lucky that I found Peet's," Baldwin said. "We probably would have done well regardless, but we would never have had the authenticity and connection with coffee that Peet's has. We would have done alright but not as great as where we are now."

PHONE CALL FROM ALFRED

When it was announced that Starbucks was being sold, Alfred immediately called Baldwin, acting surprised. Baldwin was staying at a hotel in Berkeley at the time. "It surprised me that he knew I was there. Alfred said, 'I hear that you're selling your company and keeping mine.' It was typical. He had sold his company years ago but still considered it his company."

After the sale, Alfred became a bother, "a pain in the ass," according to Baldwin. Every time he visited the main office, he'd get a royal reception, "but he also turned up in the stores and started criticizing me and Jim Reynolds in front of the employees. He bashed us and called us bureaucrats. It was inappropriate." That Alfred was hanging around in the stores and presenting himself as the man behind Peet's also led to aggravations at the main office.

In the meantime, however, Baldwin was preoccupied with the daily state of affairs and the expansion plans, so he saw Alfred rarely. Of course, Alfred no longer had an official position with the company after his consulting had ended. "He told me once that he regretted that he hadn't given the company a different name, so that his own name wouldn't have been associated with the company forever," Baldwin said. "Alfred felt mixed. He was proud of the company, but he also struggled with the fact that he was no longer in control."

It's tempting to speculate. What would have become of Starbucks if it had stayed with Peet's? Possibly, the company would have become a medium-sized coffee chain on the West Coast with strong regional ties, just like Peet's had been for almost two dozen years. That would have been in line with the way in which both companies had grown before they ended up under the same owners. Possibly, the mutual trust would have increased and that could have led, in the end, to a parting of ways and seeking of their own destinies.

For Baldwin, Starbucks was a closed chapter. Just like Bowker, he competed for a while with the company that had been founded by him. But few entrepreneurs have had a similar experience. They sparingly commented on Starbucks after they both left the company. "Starbucks developed further. I let it go," Baldwin said. "It would have been neurotic to even now get upset about the company or try to meddle with its management."

Bowker added, "Often people asked me, 'How could you ever have sold Starbucks?' But at that moment in time, it was a much smaller company. In Howard Schultz's eyes, it might have been the coffee company it has become today, but that wasn't what I was seeing then."

Siegl, who had left Starbucks much earlier, was particularly pleased that he and the company became part of the movement that exposed Americans to quality coffee: "I'm glad that Gordon,

Jerry, and I could follow in Alfred's footsteps and contribute to the development of specialty coffee." He then told me enthusiastically about new coffee firms in his neighborhood, seeing the progress taken another step further.

It's crystal clear when you are listening to the three of them that it's still about that initial spark, during that lunch decades ago when they were talking about starting a business and then suddenly realized: We share a passion for coffee.

"His mantra was, 'You do it in the best possible way, with the best coffee.'"

—Mary Williams, former senior vice president of Starbucks

8

THE TEACHER

E ven though Alfred had struggled in school, that didn't stop him from becoming an excellent teacher himself. It's remarkable how generous he was in sharing his knowledge and contacts, and how willing he was to assist coffee entrepreneurs who were starting out themselves.

When he left Peet's in the mid-eighties, Alfred had ample time and often he'd help out entrepreneurs and start-ups without asking for anything in return. After all, he didn't really need the money. The list of entrepreneurs who received some form of training from him is quite extensive. And anyone who worked with him would see business improve as a result of the association, so many coffee entrepreneurs were eager to get the kind of stamp of approval that indicated they had learned their expertise from the coffee master Alfred Peet. There's room for exaggeration here. Sal Bonavita, the second owner of Peet's, said, while laughing out loud, "If he had trained everyone who said they were trained by him, he wouldn't have had the time to roast a single coffee bean." Alfred's most famous pupils had been the three founders of Starbucks, of course, but there were others who also became quite well known. One of these is Jamie Anderson, who started a store, heavily modeled on Peet's, in Austin. Anderson considered Alfred the "godfather" of good coffee in the country. Susan O'Hori opened a similar shop in Santa Fe. Arnold Spinelli also became

a student of Alfred's and started Spinelli Coffee Roasters with
two partners, which became a chain of fourteen stores (they were
eventually acquired and, since then, they have mostly been active
in Asia). Others, like the aforementioned George Howell, simply
were inspired by Peet's in Berkeley and became influential coffee
entrepreneurs themselves.

Alfred truly enjoyed educating others about coffee. Thanks
to his far-reaching knowledge of the product and the business, he
was able to connect people through coffee, both entrepreneurs and
customers, much like a musician might do in the music industry.

The five entrepreneurs presented in this chapter still cherish
the lessons they learned from Alfred, even though these lessons
were often very challenging.

DON'T GET DISTRACTED

At the end of the eighties, Alfred met a protégé with whom he
was to have a long friendship. Her name was Mary Williams. In
the end, she became a senior vice president of Starbucks, where
for years she was responsible for the quality of the company's
coffee. Prior to that, she had a managerial role with a coffee
distributor in New York. In 1988, she came to California to start a
coffee branch for the food company Klein Brothers International.
At that time, she spoke to several people in the Bay Area and very
soon learned the name Alfred Peet. She approached him and
asked if he wanted to taste coffee with her, and he said yes.

In a telephone conversation, Williams mentioned that she
had been quite nervous because of Alfred's reputation. Her fear
seemed to have been unfounded because "from the moment I
met Alfred in person, it clicked." At the end of the day, after the

cupping of a great number of coffees and long discussions, Alfred said he knew what she was talking about, and that they could work together. "That was so typical of him—without you noticing it, he was testing you."

Just like everyone else, Williams quickly got to see Alfred's hard side. "He could be very difficult, but if you were the real thing and you were passionate about coffee and eager to learn, then he'd invest a lot of time in you. In that way, he was really quite fantastic."

She remembered one incident very clearly, and it showed the devotion that Alfred expected of everyone. "Cupping can be messy, and I grabbed some paper towels to wipe it off. He looked at me disapprovingly and said, 'Okay—are you cupping or playing the cleaning lady?' I never forgot that. When you're dealing with coffee, you shouldn't get distracted by other things."

According to Williams, she got along with Alfred because she didn't have her own company. If she had been the owner of a coffee roasting company, then his criticism might have been more hurtful. Or maybe Alfred was just milder in his treatment of women. Whatever the case, Williams felt that there hadn't been anyone in the coffee business who had built up the kind of relationship she had with Alfred. "Men had a much harder time with his criticism. But I had a different mentality. I didn't try to debate him, as many men did. I just listened to his criticism and then did my own thing," she said, laughing.

But there was another reason for the bond between the two. Williams turned out to be very talented, and Alfred respected that. "My palate is pretty well developed and I had a good nose. At the time, I was very good in the tasting and naming of coffees. Alfred was the best. In fact, I never met anyone else who was better. But for him it was nice to have someone nearby who was one of his equals in that sense."

Alfred and Williams would meet weekly for lunch. She was very passionate about coffee and wanted to change the coffee world, and Alfred thought that was great. He told her that he was glad that, after all his pioneering, the really good coffees were finally reaching a wider audience.

OPPORTUNITY KNOCKS

Williams's talent was quickly noticed by Starbucks, and they offered her a job. She hesitated to take it. The company from Seattle was still small, and she had a really good job with Klein Brothers International. Starbucks had potential but the job they had offered her was not similar to her position at Klein's. So, she called Alfred. "He said, 'If I had been younger, I'd go for that job. It's a great opportunity for you and the coffee business. You should take it.' He was the one who convinced me."

Williams moved to Seattle, and one of the first things she started with Starbucks was a training program for fifteen talented young employees. It doesn't take much guesswork to determine whom she invited to give the training. For Alfred, it was a new job as an advisor, but according to others, it was also a way for him to get back at the owners of Peet's.

The young people in the program were somewhat bashful because they had heard about Alfred's reputation. "But everyone was in awe of him," Williams said. "He knew so much about coffee. We just stood there, and it was such a joy to listen to him and learn from him." The fifteen trainees became "enormously important" for the further development of Starbucks.

Alfred taught them about the shortcomings of a coffee bean, the humidity and color of beans, the differences between the different coffee-producing countries, the curve of the roasting process, and the grinding and smelling of coffee. The young coffee professionals also overheard his debates with Starbucks CEO Howard Schultz and Mary Williams about how you can preserve the objectives of a small company even when expanding. However, the buying of coffee, the roasting, marketing, and sales—they became increasingly separate divisions within Starbucks. Alfred disapproved of that. It was important to him that a coffee entrepreneur be skilled in all aspects of the profession.

As Williams noted, Alfred's principles wouldn't be maintained by Starbucks. "Alfred couldn't compromise. His mantra was 'You do it in the best possible way, with the best coffee.' When I was at Starbucks that's what we did. I wish I could still say that for the company today. Since I've left, the coffee quality has changed so much."

In 2003, Williams left Starbucks. For a while she lived in New York City, where Alfred would visit her. Williams organized a party for him when he turned seventy-five but that didn't agree with him. "For two months, we heard nothing. He didn't like growing old and had become very depressed because of that party," Williams said, laughing. Needless to say, after that, she didn't organize any more parties for him.

"Alfred was enormously proud of his accomplishments. But he was also embarrassed by it. In many ways, he was a rather shy man. Many people described him as remote or indifferent, but I think it was shyness. When people said nice things about him, he'd get very embarrassed."

Oddly, there was one thing Alfred was not embarrassed about at all. Though it's a bizarre story, multiple people I spoke to brought it up. "When we were out to dinner," Williams recalls, "Alfred always brought the special spoon he used for cupping. Not only to taste his own coffee but also the coffee of others at the table. I will never forget the faces of other guests when Alfred, without asking for permission, stuck his spoon in their cups to taste the coffee. But then again it was Alfred Peet. He was famous in those circles and there was no one who dared object or say anything."

MASTER CLASS

There was another Dutchman in the coffee industry who sought Alfred's advice, though not to learn about the coffee business, but to offer training. Willem Boot had come to the West Coast in the late eighties while working with Probat, the famous German maker of coffee roasters. He organized workshops at the company office in San Francisco to "spread the knowledge of coffee" and invited Alfred to lend his expertise.

Boot descended from a family of coffee entrepreneurs. His father was one of the godfathers of specialty coffee in the Netherlands. Aside from the family's coffee store, run by his brother, Boot still currently owns a consulting company for coffee in San Francisco, with clients ranging from coffee-producing countries to real estate developers.

Alfred agreed to meet Boot, but they quickly clashed. At first, Alfred seemed noncommittal as to whether he was willing to provide the training. He suggested they roast some coffee first. Clearly, it was a test but it didn't make Boot nervous. "I was relatively young, but had heard a lot about roasting over the years," Boot explains.

The two Dutchmen started with a good coffee from Guatemala. The first pop was heard during the roasting. "It's going fast, I remember thinking. Pretty soon, he'll take it out." Stoically, Alfred stood next to the roaster, spoon in hand to fetch the beans and check the roasting. "But he kept on roasting. The second pop followed. I called out in surprise, 'What are you doing? You're burning that coffee! You can't do that!'" It was an awkward situation. "He looked at me with an expression that seemed to say, 'Who do you think you are that you can tell me how to roast coffee?'" Boot explained to Alfred that he had never roasted coffee that dark, or "maybe once . . . by mistake." In his view, taste and nuance would get lost with such a dark roast. Of course, Alfred was initially annoyed, but they were able to move past the early tension and have a very open discussion, after which they proceeded to taste coffee all day, not even taking a break for lunch.

At the end of the day, Alfred committed to the training, but under one condition: He needed a couple of days to get everything ready, indicating that he took teaching very seriously. But that devotion was appreciated, and people still tell Boot how much they learned from Alfred.

During that first meeting, Boot realized Alfred was a difficult man. "He could be very charming, but he could also express himself rather fiercely. I recognized that, because my father was quite similar in the way he taught people."

Alfred was inclined to challenge people and put them in their place, Boot added. Sometimes that irritated Boot, and he'd provoke Alfred and ask him if he enjoyed being so difficult. Alfred answered, "This is the way I work. It's very intense. But it's the best thing there is."

According to Boot, Alfred was very talented in his approach to coffee. "I think this had to do with his background in tea. He was a very good taster. But he also really focused on dark roasts. That was his style and I've often wondered whether he'd be just as good with lighter roasts," which Boot prefers.

In spite of all the changes in the coffee market, "Alfred never fell off his pedestal for me," Boot admitted. "I've always held him in the highest regard. Especially because he was such a purist."

EXACTING STANDARDS

One of the Boot trainees was Joe Paff, who now has his own coffee store (Gold Rush Coffee) in Eureka, California. But Paff had already met Alfred before he took the training. "Our friendship started when he asked me what the first coffee was that I really liked. When I said Sulawesi, Alfred became very excited, and he told me he was the first person in California who had bought and roasted that coffee."

Paff said that Alfred hated any pompous terms to describe coffee and he demanded that his students avoid pretentiousness. "People tend to do that when cupping, but he called coffee an 'experience of the senses,' and you need to use the proper words to express those experiences."

To Alfred, if it were true, it would do. It could even be outlandish, as long as it was true. To support his point, Alfred used a bizarre example. If, he said, the taste of the coffee reminds you of your grandmother's cupboard, then it tastes like your grandmother's cupboard. The comparison made Paff laugh. When tasting tea, it was the same story. When they told Alfred that they were pouring him a Darjeeling, he took a sip and said that it didn't match up: "I'd never see a beautiful woman when I drink a Darjeeling. This must be an Assam."

Alfred also had a fine nose for wine, and he liked to prank people during wine tastings to debunk the wine snobbery that sometimes occurred at such tastings. People often gave him expensive bottles, like Château Lafite-Rothschild and wines from other renowned labels. "He'd replace it with a good Cab, reattach the cork and loved to make fun of people who were thinking they were drinking a bottle worth $500." He believed that whatever the label said, you always have to taste blind and decide upon quality that way. "No need to be pretentious about it," Paff said.

Alfred also told Paff to run his fingers through the green coffee beans when opening a bag, prior to roasting. "My body would experience a sensation for which there might not be any words. Your senses can teach you stuff that eludes your thoughts or that you cannot put into words," he said.

Alfred showed that he not only had a very high standard for coffee but also for food. Once Alfred and his girlfriend at the time visited Paff. "She told me how he had thrown out her entire spice rack, because the spices weren't fresh enough. There was no one at the time who cared about that sort of thing. Now that's different. The beautiful thing of the current coffee culture, which he started, is that we're not only more aware of the quality of coffee, but we're also more aware of the quality of other things, such as herbs, spices, vegetables, meat, and eggs."

You could argue that Alfred displayed a certain arrogance because his demands for quality were greater than those of others. But people didn't see it that way, mostly because he did it with "humor and good intentions," according to Paff. His high standards were often remembered with a smile, both by employees and friends. A well-known anecdote recounts how Alfred explained to his employees the proper way to close the door of the shop. It seemed trivial, but employees had to endure these endless "door instructions" time and again.

Paff further remembered how an employee called him once in a panic because there was a "crazy guy" in the store who had asked for a screwdriver because he wanted to open the espresso machine. "I knew immediately—that must be Alfred." The employee was told to hand over the screwdriver, and Alfred then disassembled the entire espresso machine to show how to clean it. "After that, he made an espresso and said, 'See! That's how you make an espresso!' You could be offended, but I didn't see it that way. There was always a great seriousness about him. He took your life more seriously than you did yourself and you had to conclude: He's right—that's how I should do it."

COFFEE DAUGHTER

"Start a coffee business now? There are so many. I don't recommend it." This was strange advice for Leigh McDonald in 1995. She had summoned her courage and called Alfred to ask him for advice on starting a coffee business in the Netherlands. He had become one of her heroes during her previous work at Starbucks on the West Coast. But there was one thing she didn't know about Alfred: "When he heard I was planning to open my business in the Netherlands, he immediately switched to Dutch. 'Oh, darling! You live in the Netherlands?' I was completely taken by surprise and did my best to answer in awkward Dutch. I had no idea he came from the Netherlands."

In the mid-nineties, McDonald went to the Netherlands on vacation, and she was offered a job in the coffee business.

Ultimately, she decided to start her own espresso bar, Coffee Connection in Amsterdam. It was for this reason she had originally contacted Alfred.

McDonald comes from Seattle, and when she was a child, her mother often took her to Starbucks at Pike Place. "My mother was immediately sold. She was a coffee fan all the way. And I loved that shop for its European feel and exotic aroma."

When she started in the Netherlands, she already had a lot of experience. Thanks to her work at Starbucks and a period in Italy, she had learned a great deal about coffee. "But I didn't have any experience roasting," she said. So, I flew to the United States, to San Francisco, to get some training. Coffee was booming everywhere. She called Jerry Baldwin and Alfred to help her get ahead. "I thought, 'What have I got to lose?' Luckily, everyone received me with open arms."

Alfred was seventy-five at the time, and he did express his skepticism about the developments in the coffee business. That's why he had originally discouraged her. "He felt the market had gone in the wrong direction. He liked small and cozy, which is typically Dutch in my opinion."

Nonetheless, he was thrilled when the young American came from the Netherlands to ask for his advice. "He took me in and often called me his 'coffee daughter.' It was remarkable how similar our lives were. He came from the Netherlands to the United States and started a European-style coffee store there, which I, as an American, intended to bring back to the Netherlands."

When she started with Coffee Connection (no ties to George Howell's business) in the Netherlands, the market was wide open. "A Dutch espresso was weak and watery. Customers didn't know what a caffè latte was. That's very different now."

After the initial phone call, the two immediately visited several coffee roasting companies in the Bay Area which Alfred had helped along. "I thought he was a modest man, and you could have a good laugh with him, especially when he started poking fun at my Dutch."

MARLON BRANDO

A month after their first meeting, McDonald returned to the United States and started her training with Alfred at a roastery in Emeryville. For three weeks, from early in the morning to late at night, they worked together. "It was a very special experience, as if you're learning yoga from a yogi in India or taking acting lessons from Marlon Brando." But Alfred was a disciplinarian: One morning he scolded her for being late. "After a strict and disciplined day of roasting and cupping coffee with Alfred, my head was so full I could barely process it all."

Alfred taught her what she had to look for in a blend. "It's about a harmony and synergy of the different elements. He explained how I had to measure the body of the coffee, and its acidity. Those two had to be in balance, both warm and cold." It struck her that Alfred was very down-to-earth when he talked about coffee. "He advised me to use fewer words. When I became too lyrical, he became impatient. He said, 'Evaluate the coffee, and decide if it's useful to your goal; don't try to top Shakespeare!'"

At the roaster, McDonald asked Alfred the question everyone asked in the beginning: When do the beans come out? "Alfred said, 'Listen to the beans; they will let you know when they are ready.'" He always had a twinkle in his eye when he said that sort of thing, but if she took the beans out too early, he'd abruptly correct her.

"Alfred was fearless. It didn't matter to him whether people liked him or not. He didn't care one bit. But he could afford to be that way, because he was such a craftsman." All in all, the experience with Alfred was unique. "I realized how fortunate I was to be mentored by such an icon of the coffee industry."

COFFEE FATHER

During one of his family trips to the Netherlands, Alfred also visited McDonald. The two drove to the village of the Lage Vuursche where McDonald had a Probat roaster. "Alfred loved the surroundings. We were driving through a tunnel of trees. The roaster was in a small barn opposite the castle of Drakensteyn."

McDonald recalls, "After our arrival, Alfred inspected the roaster and started sighing and complaining. The machine wasn't clean enough for Alfred and, because of that, the air intake was compromised." She knew about Alfred's precision and emphasis on maintenance. "According to him, it was a mess. I think that was the first time he was really disappointed with me. The condition of the roaster didn't meet his high standards, and he disapproved of my roasting coffee on it. We had to clean everything first."

This was followed by another disappointment. "We were at the Coffee Connection, tasting coffees, but when some customers came in, I explained what we were doing. Alfred became quite angry with me because I became distracted from my task. People had to stay away when you were tasting coffee, that was his belief." It was typical of his black-and-white way of thinking, she said. "He simply didn't understand how you could combine the two."

McDonald noticed that her "coffee father," as she liked to call him in return, became more distant. "He pushed me away and that hurt. I wasn't fully ignored, but there was a cooling off of the relationship."

However, they kept working together and Alfred helped her to develop the first coffee blend for Coffee Connection. "It was a blend with a very unusual coffee: a Bugisu, from Uganda," McDonald explained. It wasn't easy to maintain the same quality, especially because there was unrest in Uganda, so then McDonald developed her own blends. "Still today I think of Alfred's advice: The synergy of the coffees must yield a better end result than each individual coffee."

When Coffee Connection had four shops, McDonald decided to sell the espresso bars. She is still fully immersed in the coffee business via her roasting and consulting company 7grams, and she's also involved in a Balinese coffee company (Munduk Coffee) and teaches yoga. "Over the years, I've developed several roasting styles, as requested by my private label customers. Recently, I made an organic dark roast," she told me. "That was an ode to my mentor Alfred. When I drink that coffee, I'm back on the West Coast, side by side at the sample roaster with Alfred."

WITHOUT COMPROMISE

Until his death, Alfred shared his knowledge with coffee professionals. His last disciple was Shirin Moayyad, who was responsible for buying coffee for Peet's in 2005. She came from Spinelli Coffee (also inspired by Alfred) and had worked for a coffee roasting company in Papua New Guinea. When she arrived at Peet's, Jerry Baldwin suggested she make a pilgrimage to the founder of the company. When she finally got around to doing that, Alfred was too weak to receive her, so they stayed in touch by phone, fax, and email instead.

Moayyad sent Alfred samples of coffee beans and asked him to taste them at home. "He then sent me his conclusions, via fax, and when I had read those, we'd follow up by phone." She remembered the handwritten reports he sent via fax. "He had beautiful handwriting. He believed in the art of calligraphy and thought that was important."

The evaluations were "spot on," according to Moayyad. "Normally, your palate deteriorates as you get older, but you didn't notice that with him." With a sample of Colombian coffee, Alfred even discovered that two almost-identical coffees had been mixed. "It's astounding that someone can taste that at the age of eighty-seven," she said.

During conversations, which focused solely on coffee, Alfred's character and temperament seemed intact as well. "He wasn't at all interested in what others might be thinking of him. He was without compromise. The only thing he cared about was the quality of the coffee," Moayyad said. She was deeply impressed by him and called him a "maestro" and "the king of our industry."

Moayyad, who now works with Nespresso on a team that is tasked with building out the coffee knowledge of the company, said that Alfred's lessons have stayed with her. "He taught me that if you're without compromise in your vision and goal of quality, that success will follow naturally." Just like her mentor, she wants to rely on her own instincts and vision: "To me, Alfred was the proof that this is the only right way."

Not all of Alfred's lessons were easy to follow, and in particular, his thoughts on the expansion of a coffee company stirred up some doubts within Moayyad (as with others before her). With the amount of coffee that was sold at Peet's, it was impossible to have the buying and roasting done by the same people, she argued. "But that vision, too, was part of the lack of compromise Alfred believed in. It was because of that that Alfred felt a company shouldn't become too big."

In a 2001 interview in the *San Francisco Chronicle*, Alfred summarized it once more: "I'd rather see a thousand fellows running their own stores than what we have now." Clearly, he was referring to coffee chains with hundreds or even thousands of stores. "If I wasn't so old, I'd open a small store and scour the world for the very best coffee you could find."

"He wanted to expand back then, but didn't want to lose control."

—Jerry Baldwin, cofounder Starbucks, boardmember Peet's

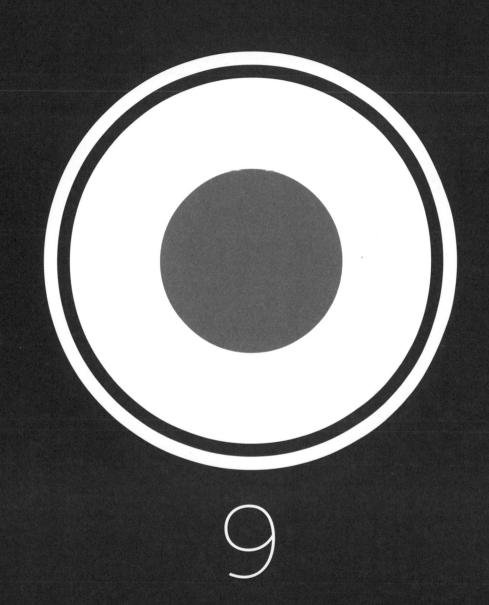

9

GROWING AND GROWING

t was to be expected. But when it happened, it still came as a shock for Peet's. When Starbucks was sold in 1987, part of the deal was that for the next four years it wouldn't expand to the Bay Area, the home market for Peet's. But barely four years later, Starbucks opened its first store in San Francisco.

Jim Reynolds, who was the roastmaster for Peet's at the time, said, "With the arrival of Starbucks, it was for the first time that another, large coffee chain established itself in the home market of Peet's, and this was a competitor with a lot of capital." Soon, there were six Starbucks stores in the Bay Area. Reynolds said that the move of the competitor irritated him at the time. "I knew Howard Schultz very well. He always considered Jerry a role model. Jerry made him into who he was. The way in which they came to the San Francisco Bay Area was rather aggressive, and I didn't like it. I got over it, later on." But Reynolds also noted that there was still plenty of room to grow for other coffee stores. The profit margins for coffee stores were still very good at that time.

A year after Peet's had to deal with this, Gordon Bowker came back on board. "At that point, things were more flexible in my life, and I missed the coffee business," he said about his return to the company. Bowker focused on the "interesting problems" that Peet's had to deal with, one of which was the rising rivalry with Starbucks. Nowadays, he looks back on it rather pragmatically:

"At Starbucks they were simply exercising their duty to their share-holders." When he returned to Peet's in 1992, Bowker became a member of the board, and he also invested in the company.

The same year, Starbucks went public. At that time, the company had 165 shops. When Peet's went public in 2001, the company had 59 stores, while Starbucks had 3,500 in the same year.

Baldwin has said that Peet's could never grow at the same pace as Starbucks. He remembered a conversation he had with Alfred about it when Alfred was still the owner. "He proposed at a dinner at his house that Peet's could merge with Starbucks and become a company like Tchibo," Baldwin said, referring to the German coffee company with hundreds of stores. "Alfred wanted to expand back then but didn't want to lose control. But when you start something like Tchibo, then you're in your office all day long, and you'll never see a single coffee bean again. I was too inexperienced to respond to Alfred's proposal, and even now, it's more than I could possibly handle. We realized at that dinner that we simply couldn't do it, and then had another glass of wine."

MARKETING VERSUS PRODUCT

According to Reynolds, Starbucks and Peet's were so different at the end of the eighties, it was inevitable that the two companies would have to part ways, developmentally. Even when he first arrived at Peet's, he had already noticed the difference between the two companies: Starbucks was a cult brand and Peet's was the favorite of coffee connoisseurs. Those identities became even stronger over time. "And that's the big difference between the two companies for me. Howard's into marketing and Jerry's focus is on the product," Reynolds said.

CEO Howard Schultz was very clued into the zeitgeist when he called Starbucks "the third place"—a living place between the office and home, a living space outside of the home. There was a whole new generation of coffee drinkers who connected with that. This was reflected in popular culture, with sitcoms such as *Friends* (1994–2004), in which a close-knit group habitually gathered in a coffee shop. The desire to buy beans and make coffee at home went down. In 2001, half of the revenue at Peet's still consisted of selling beans, but for Starbucks those sales had become much less important. And they continued to expand, sometimes even building more than one Starbucks on the same block. Peet's grew more gradually. Even after they went public, there wasn't a big expansion. When they went public they gained a little under $30 million, two-thirds of which were destined for the company itself. The rest went to existing shareholders who sold their shares. Peet's was listed on the Nasdaq Stock Market, the stock market for tech companies, which also lists other companies that don't really seem to belong there.

There are several reasons for a company to go public. Shareholders may want to cash in their ownership holdings of the company, or the company may need to acquire extra money for expansion or reduction of debt. For Peet's, those all seemed valid. Shareholders like Baldwin and Bowker wanted to cash in. But Peet's also had debts, and by going public that issue was largely resolved, giving the company more room to grow—and there was plenty of space to grow in the coffee market at the time.

When Peet's went public, specialty coffee occupied a third of the total US coffee market, and it was the fastest growing market segment. According to the National Coffee Association, revenues in 2001 were something like $18.5 billion, which was a dramatic increase from $13 billion in 1993.

A DUTCH AUCTION

Peet's going public happened through a so-called Dutch auction. This means that the price per share is determined by bids that investors make in advance. If there's a lot of demand, or if investors think the company is worth more, then the price per share will shoot up. Search engine Google, for example, opted for the same kind of Dutch auction years after Peet's went public and saw its share price skyrocket due to its perceived worth. For Peet's, the Dutch auction was disappointing: The company hoped to fetch $10 to $14 dollars per share, but it ended up being just $8 per share. That said, the price of shares did go up the very first day.

For the first time, outsiders could see in great detail how the company had done in previous years, because once a company goes public, it must become fully transparent. In 2000, the company had $85 million in revenue and a net loss of $2.3 million. In comparison, Starbucks, in the same year, had an annual revenue of $2.2 billion.

After that, Peet's improved: In 2001, the loss was converted into a small profit and the revenue went up 12 percent. It's interesting to see how they made their numbers that year. While most of their revenue still came from the stores, the fastest revenue growth (40 percent) came when Peet's started selling coffee beans and coffee to supermarkets and offices. Peet's built its own distribution network for this, which was an expensive method, but one that turned out to be very useful and which made competitors jealous.

Today, Peet's has six hundred trucks that deliver coffee to

about fourteen thousand supermarkets. The company puts the packages on the shelves itself and it has some say in the presentation of the coffee. What would Alfred have thought of that? In the past, he had prevented distribution to supermarkets because he feared that the quality of the coffee would suffer. But with the method (and control) that Peet's had chosen to distribute to supermarkets, as well as improvements in packaging that prolonged the freshness of the coffee on the shelves, the margin of error for failure became much slimmer.

The year 2005 was a good one for Peet's, highlighted by the opening of twenty new stores. The revenue growth that year was 22.5 percent and profits climbed to $8.8 million. Peet's wasn't a mere Bay Area institution anymore, but could be found everywhere along the West Coast, from Seattle to Los Angeles. Just as Starbucks had initially stayed away from the Bay Area, Peet's originally did the same with Seattle. By the time Peet's arrived in Seattle, it hardly made a difference to the now-giant Starbucks.

In the meantime, Baldwin had stepped down from the leadership team at Peet's to take on a supervisory role, just like Bowker had when he joined the board. In 2008, however, Bowker retired. At that point, the company was run by Chris Mottern (who formerly worked with Capri Sun), followed by Patrick O'Dea (Archway/Mother's Cookies, Stella Foods, and Procter & Gamble).

In the coffee roasting part of the company itself, business remained virtually unchanged. Reynolds was still the roastmaster and responsible for the quality of the coffee, even though he had gained a new pupil by the name of Doug Welsh.

A HIGH COFFEE PRICE

Growing a coffee chain like Peet's is one thing, but controlling the price of coffee beans is quite another. In the annual report of 2011, CEO O'Dea was happy with the results "despite record-high coffee costs since becoming a public company." That was not an understatement. The price of coffee had risen greatly, from about $0.40 per American pound to almost $3. But it should be noted that in 2001, when Peet's went public, the price of coffee had been at a record low, after a period in which the market had been inundated with coffee.

The price of coffee is determined by a number of factors. A deal can be made between provider and buyer, and a batch of coffee can be auctioned off on the Internet, but when one refers to the "price of coffee," one has to think of the transactions being carried out at the coffee exchange. Various cities have these exchanges, but the one in New York City is the most important one: Coffee has been traded there since 1882. The New York Board of Trade is the primary trading center for coffee; in 2007 it was acquired and integrated into the Intercontinental Exchange (ICE).

The standard for the coffee price in New York is a C-Contract, a unit to determine the price of arabica beans. Robusta beans are traded separately, at prices determined by the London exchange. If you look at a table of the coffee price (the C-Contract) over time, you'll see some wild fluctuations.

A well-known panic in the coffee market occurred in 1994, when Brazil—at the time responsible for a quarter of worldwide coffee production—was hit twice by a severe frost. About 40 percent of the harvest was lost, and buyers of Brazilian coffee had to switch quickly to different providers. This led to a tripling of the coffee price.

Alfred was a coffee trader in the years after he left Peet's. Investing in coffee was a hobby for him, without it ever becoming a serious source of income. Family members remember how elated he was that coffee he had bought in Indonesia had doubled in price on its way to Europe, enabling him to sell the entire batch before it had even arrived. He must have handled his orders through a local office and intermediary, and he would have been able to read on the financial pages of the newspaper whether or not he had earned anything.

Nowadays, trade happens electronically, and one can check the price of coffee on a smartphone, but as far as the actual trade goes, little has changed. It starts with sellers and buyers making a deal. Coffee companies (roasters, exporters, traders) can make a short-term transaction with direct payment, but it can also happen on a long-term basis with a fixed price that is set for a certain upcoming date.

It was exactly for that reason that Alfred, in the period with Sal Bonavita, put in the $300,000 coffee order. He made that deal, not to get the coffee delivered at once or because it was a bargain, but to ensure that high-quality coffee would always be in-house at a certain price. The lack of a certain kind of coffee might mean that a popular blend could not be sold anymore. That could be a disaster for the customers and the company.

But a deal like that can also be a risk. When, for example, a coffee roasting company signs a contract for delivery in the future and knows what will be paid, there's always a chance that the coffee price will have gone down by the moment of delivery. On the other hand, it may have gone up, so it can be both an advantage and a disadvantage. But, of course, no one wants to run the risk of being disadvantaged. The containment of this risk is achieved as follows.

Parties that trade in coffee do this at the exchange. They agree upon term contracts, so-called futures, which can be traded at the exchange like those in New York and London, and this paper trade determines the price of coffee. When the coffee has to be delivered to the coffee roasting company, the term contract expires and the bill is settled.

If a coffee roasting company is smart, any advantage or disadvantage in the contract will be mitigated by the result of the term contract. That's how one tries to arrive at a degree of price stability. In this way, a coffee roasting company can calculate a stable price to those parties who buy from them—so the knife cuts both ways.

A CENTURIES-OLD TRADITION

Working with term contracts is a centuries-old tradition that was invented in Amsterdam during the time of the Dutch East India Company. These contracts were drafted for, among other things, the arrival of spices from the Dutch East Indies. The contracts were negotiated on a bridge near the current Central Station, an open-air space often seen as the first financial market (exchange) in the world.

Term contracts and supplemental financial products such as options (the right to buy a term contract) stimulate trade in a product such as coffee and, according to market laws, set the best possible price for the product. But the paper trade also attracts investors who are only interested in profit from trading in these contracts. That can make the market more unstable and lead to sharp fluctuations in coffee price. At the same time, those parties ensure that there can be sufficient trade and that others are able to create price stability for their own companies.

In the last few decades, the role of the exchange has weakened. Coffee-producing countries have tried to control the price, after the example of OPEC, the Organization of the Petroleum Exporting Countries. But they haven't been very successful thus far. Furthermore, big coffee companies often deal directly with coffee producers. They need such big quantities of coffee that insufficient supply is, in fact, the greatest risk.

In addition, the Internet has reinforced the ability of coffee buyers to get in direct contact with coffee producers. Take, for example, the Cup of Excellence, a competition that is held in several countries, in which coffee producers can send in their harvests for judgment. Such competitions have been happening in the agricultural world for centuries; for example, harvest parties crown winners who can then charge a higher price for their produce. What's different, however, is that the acclaimed coffees of the Cup of Excellence now can be sold all over the world through the Internet, rather than just locally. At online auctions, prices will shoot up on a regular basis. Especially in Asia, people pay top dollar for special award-winning coffees.

But even with all the attempts to try and manage the price, Mother Nature still has the biggest impact on price. In 2014, the price of coffee went up 50 percent, due to a drought in Brazil as well as leaf rust, a plant disease that destroyed part of the coffee harvest in Central America. The year after that, the price went down again. The cause? It was raining again in Brazil.

NEW GROWTH IMPULSE

Peet's grew slowly, but they managed to grow at moments when the higher price of coffee was a problem for the competition. The value of its shares followed the same trajectory. Things changed a few years after O'Dea had expressed his worry about the price of coffee. Suddenly, there was a buyer with a Dutchman at the wheel, and he saw possibilities to enhance the business and make it more competitive.

"I devoted all my time to the company, so I neglected my personal life."

—Alfred Peet

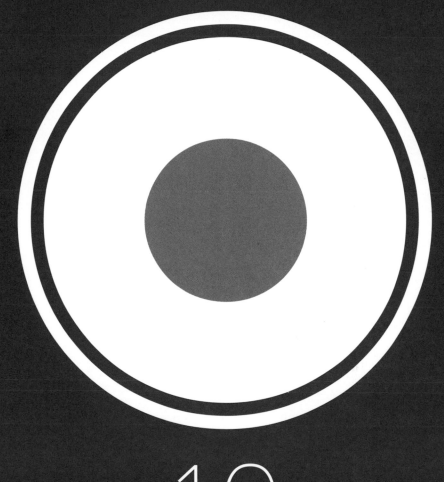

10

ALFRED'S QUEST

lfred always traveled a lot for work, but starting in the mid-eighties when he no longer had a role at Peet's, his appetite for travel increased. He decided to do a cruise that would take him from the West Coast to Alaska and the southernmost tip of Chile. Other destinations were remarkable, too. He booked trips to China, Tibet, Russia, Mongolia, and Uzbekistan. He came back with the usual stories about natural beauty and impressive tourist attractions, but there were other things that he had noticed.

"The Russians were bitter, but I would be, too, if I had to stand in line for food every day. What a difference with Tashkent and Uzbekistan. The people were totally different there, very vivacious. There were large markets with many vegetables and fruits, all local products. There was enough and good food, and that must be the difference." In Ulaanbaatar, in Mongolia, where he went in the early eighties, Alfred was worried about air pollution. "There was a big coal plant with lots of emissions. I pitied the people who lived there. They used to have clean air and now they were polluting all of it."

In China, the group Alfred had traveled with suddenly noticed that he had gone missing. He had walked into a tea shop and by using his hands and feet, he had told them what he wanted. The seller quickly realized he was an expert, and he took Alfred to a back room where the really special tea was. Back in the bus, he shared his enthusiasm with his fellow travelers: "Look at that beautiful tea—you have to buy some!"

Alfred's house was filled with objects that he bought during his trips. They were beautiful, from Chinese masks to teapots and statues.

Alfred could have aged gracefully in Berkeley. He lived in that nice house on Keith Street, and Berkeley was (and is) spacious and calm, without being boring like some other suburbs in the East Bay. That is partly because of the students and UC Berkeley— they keep the city lively. The climate in the Bay Area is pleasant, which was another reason Alfred started his business there.

When family members came over from Holland, he often took them out sailing. One of the highlights was sailing under the Golden Gate Bridge. Until late in life, Alfred remained active. He biked around Sausalito and went for hikes in the Napa Valley. To his friends' and family's shock, he also decided to go bungee jumping when he was well over seventy.

He also liked to attend classical music concerts in San Francisco. He read a lot; his house was filled with books and newspapers, and he had a book stand from which he would read while eating. He had friends over for dinner regularly, like Bonnie Grossman and her husband, who lived nearby. And he continued to mentor coffee entrepreneurs. His fame had crossed borders, and European entrepreneurs often sent him beans with the request to assess them.

Alfred was the epitome of the businessman who had "made it"—a man who did whatever he wanted to do. But underneath the surface, things were eating at him.

DEVOTEE

"I devoted all my time to the company, so I neglected my personal life," Alfred said in a conversation with the author Adah Bakalinsky in the early eighties. "Everything was about the company. Now that the company is gone, the healthy stress is gone too . . . and then I'm talking about the engagement with your own company and the pleasure it gives you. I looked in the mirror and said to myself, 'There's still a lot I need to do and learn.'"

When he left the Netherlands, Alfred had remained Catholic, but that changed over time. He joined the Unitarian Church, a religion that sees God as one entity, as opposed to the Trinity (Father, Son, and Holy Ghost) of the Catholic Church. In Berkeley, in the sixties, there were all sorts of spiritual lifestyles, and like many other people, Alfred shopped around. There was a time when he meditated every morning, but he also decorated his house with rosaries.

He was interested in Zen Buddhism, possibly because of his interest in China and other tea countries. For a while, he stayed at a Zen Center in Berkeley. The book that he studied there is heavily underlined and filled with notes. The book later ended up in the hands of Ross Blum, a fellow Zen Buddhist, and former (longtime) employee of Peet's on Vine Street. "When I saw him, I wanted to talk about it with him, but he didn't want to." The book can now be seen at the Vine Street store.

However, visits to a therapist and a summer painting class with the California Institute of the Arts couldn't pacify Alfred's inner turmoil. To his surprise, he developed an ulcer in the eighties. "I should have had that much earlier, when I was busy with my company!" But the doctor's explanation seemed plausible to him: It was a delayed response to all the stress he had experienced as the owner of Peet's. He was laughing about this in his conversation with Bakalinsky.

From there, the conversation seemed to have turned into therapy. "All the things I got from my father and mother I left far behind me.

There's little left of anything of them that means anything to me," he stated rather somberly. A few moments later in the conversation, there was another painful insight: "I can't seem to make a direct connection with people and that scares me. In essence, that's what's going on. I fear intimacy. I run from it."

And yet, there were many friendships, which would last until his death, such as the ones with Jim Reynolds and his wife, and Grossman and her husband. According to friends and family, he dated many women and later regretted (as he mentioned in a 1984 newspaper interview) that he never married. Why it didn't work out is guesswork, but Alfred's confession of fearing intimacy may be a valid reason. He said it at a point in time when almost no one knew about Judy . . .

FAMILY TIES

Sometime in 1984, John Weaver walked into the office at Peet's, and what he saw there took him by surprise. "Alfred was crying in the hallway—he had a picture in his hand. I had never seen him like that." The picture was of a young woman: Alfred's daughter. Almost no one around him knew of the existence of Judy, who, at her birth, was put up for adoption.

"They really look alike, Judy and Alfred," family members of Alfred's in the Netherlands had said before I met her. When Judy McCall started talking in her father's first store on Vine Street, there was a resolve about her that also was a direct reflection of Alfred. There seemed to be no need to smooth out the wrinkles from the past, and she made jokes with an undertone that seemed to suggest "How could he ever have done that!"

"We do indeed resemble each other. We also have the same facial expressions," McCall said, explaining that she grew up in a family where all the children were adopted, which meant that they didn't resemble each other at all. "For me that was very confusing. To then understand things about someone, without having to think about it, like with my dad—that was really new to me. It was a shock."

There are multiple speculations as to why Alfred and his then-girlfriend decided to offer their daughter up for adoption. He wanted to marry his girlfriend, but she declined, some say. Others said he was the one who backed off. On top of that, a lot of things were happening at the same time for him, McCall explained. "He said a couple of times that he wasn't able to get married, become a dad, and lead a company. That was too much. Because of that, I was put up for adoption."

After her birth in 1968, she ended up with adoptive parents in Bakersfield, about 280 miles south of San Francisco. Oil and agriculture were the most important industries there. "It was a very conservative environment to grow up in and very unimaginative compared to Berkeley."

INSTANT COFFEE FOR ALFRED

When she was eighteen, McCall decided to contact her biological parents. She was successful in doing so because they had, at the time, given their permission for their daughter to contact them. McCall wrote her mother a letter and in the subsequent phone call, she heard her father's name for the first time. Alfred didn't hesitate one moment when he heard about the contact and learned where McCall lived. The very next day he called her, and the day after that, he was on a plane to Bakersfield.

"When Alfred arrived, he received instant coffee because that's what we always drank at home. He didn't say a word, but the following Christmas, he sent me two pounds of coffee and a French press to make my coffee," she said, laughing.

"I think he imagined that everything would be wonderful and fabulous. The idea of the daughter who embraces the long-lost father. As if he were the part that I would have missed my entire life. But that's not what happened." And that was tough, according to McCall. "My relationship with him would always be strained. Whenever he had problems with people—and that was often—his attitude triggered the ending of the relationship with those people. With us you couldn't do that of course. We were stuck with each other."

McCall continued, "What must have been awkward for him is that there was someone who understood him like no one else did. He was a very private person, very cautious with people, always wondering what people wanted from him." It had to do with his position in Berkeley and the Bay Area, McCall realized later. "He was famous but I didn't really know that back then. When I went to college there were fellow students who spoke admiringly of 'Mr. Peet.' Everyone always had a very high opinion of him. And I thought: Really? Him?"

SILENCING

A year after the first meeting with Alfred, the two went to the Netherlands to meet the rest of the family. McCall met two cousins and their families, and Hetty and Gertrude, Alfred's sisters. Her Dutch grandmother had died by that time. It struck her that they were all in great shape. "They went hiking and biking a lot. As an American woman, I wasn't as fit as them and my father liked to rub it in."

She also remembered a conflict between her father and his sister, Gertrude. "They were arguing about a tree in the garden, and it ended with Gertrude telling him to bugger off and leave her alone. That was the first time that I saw someone who stood up to him." Others in the family were very familiar with this pattern: Alfred wouldn't be silenced by anyone, but his older sister could handle him.

McCall liked being with the family in the Netherlands, but she noticed that Alfred became more and more disgruntled. "I wasn't allowed to walk around with my hands in my pockets, he didn't let me drink alcohol because 'I'd become an alcoholic,' and he wanted me to be productive, even at night. He even encouraged me to read German with Gertrude. That I didn't speak any other language and that I hadn't traveled much, like the rest of his family, he thought was odd."

But on one level, Alfred had to concede that his daughter outperformed him. Besides being an elementary school teacher, she was a professional musician and played the cello. When she was in the Netherlands with her dad, she and Gertrude played together, as Gertrude could play the flute and the piano. As a great lover of music, Alfred had tried to play an instrument like the cello or flute, but he had been unsuccessful.

McCall also saw the generous side of her dad during her trip. "My cousin Rudolf and his family didn't have a dryer, and he thought that was ridiculous, so he bought one for them. He didn't want to talk about it; he just did it. And he did it often . . . certain impulses showing great generosity."

McCall still lives on the West Coast, slightly north of San Francisco, working as a teacher and a cellist. Her husband is a musician, too, and plays contrabass in jazz ensembles. When I was saying goodbye to her, she proudly showed me a picture of her two kids.

According to Bonnie Grossman, Alfred was very fond of his daughter's mother. That no family came of it, but an adoption and two parents who separated, will undoubtedly have had its effect, even though Alfred didn't show it. Yet, some former regrets did seem to come to the surface when, in 1976, his nephew Joost van der Flier visited him with his then-pregnant wife Janneke. While Joost had gone on a Yellowstone camping trip with Alfred previously, Janneke hadn't met Alfred yet.

"He was very ambivalent with me, as if he were envious of us being married," she said. "I felt uncomfortable when at one point he wanted to touch my stomach. Only later, when Alfred visited the Netherlands with Judy, did I realize how difficult that visit must have been."

Right after the birth of their daughter, Alfred sent Janneke and Joost some clothes. "They were three very pretty dresses, from the ages of six months to two years. I was surprised he had bought them. Maybe they had been sitting inside his house all along?"

VISIT TO AMSTERDAM

During a stay in the Netherlands in 2002, Alfred ended up in the hospital because of worsening prostate problems. He was in Amsterdam, having been invited by Starbucks, shortly after the company had opened a large coffee roasting facility near the Amsterdam harbor.

Chris Jordan, who was responsible for the coffee quality at Starbucks at the time, had asked Alfred to come for a training of some young coffee roasters. He had learned a lot from Alfred during the training that Starbucks Vice President Mary Williams had established in Seattle. "I was completely overwhelmed by his knowledge and experience at the time."

The intention was that Alfred had come to inspire them. The first day of class, they were completely smitten. "It was as if he were coming full circle. He had brought great coffee to the West

Coast by his way of roasting coffee, and now he had come to share that in the Netherlands," Jordan said.

Alfred stayed with Jordan and his family, and during the night he was in a lot of pain. Jordan took him to the hospital, and a few hours later, he drove to the roasting facility. To his surprise, Alfred showed up at seven o'clock in the morning. "At the hospital, they didn't know he had left—he hadn't checked out or anything. It was crazy to do something like that after having been taken in during the night, but Alfred was so stubborn." The second day of the training was fine and even though he had been in the hospital, he managed to mesmerize everyone again, according to Jordan, who would later become CEO of the coffee company Verve in Santa Cruz.

FRANCE?

When Alfred was in Amsterdam for the training, he had already suggested to Jordan that he was considering moving back to the Netherlands. He weighed the possibilities of relocation with his family and considered places such as Bergen, in the province of Noord-Holland, where his mother had lived until her death in 1976. But converting his US citizenship was not easy and Alfred decided against it.

He also considered moving to France where his niece Mariette Merle and her husband have a vineyard near Hyères, on the Mediterranean coast, not far from Marseilles. "He thought it was great we had started our own company," Merle explained. "It meant he hadn't been the only entrepreneur in the family." Alfred visited her for the first time in 1997 and gave her all sorts of advice as to how to run her company. He came back several times and called her to give more advice. "We had plans to expand, and he wanted to know everything about it."

And while Alfred didn't have any plans to start his own vineyard, he wouldn't have been the first coffee entrepreneur to become a winemaker—Jerry Baldwin had purchased a vineyard in the Sonoma Valley, mostly producing Zinfandels. Alfred was, however, very interested in his niece's company Domaine Bouisse Matteri and the way in which Mariette had become an entrepreneur. Needless to say, the climate of southern France was very appealing, too.

"He had great doubts. Alfred really wanted to return to Europe," his niece said. At the same time, in his conversations with Merle, she also noticed he had cultivated an image of the Netherlands that was stuck in the forties and fifties—the time of his departure. "He started realizing that Europe had changed and was wondering whether he could still fit in after having lived on the American West Coast for so many years."

The family advised him to rent an apartment in Hyères to see if he liked it. Up until then, he had always stayed with Merle, but that became awkward, as Alfred always did his own thing, in his own way: "He was rather strange, almost maniacal about things. All clothes had to be neatly arranged in the closets. We had a house with kids, dogs and cats, so you can imagine he was kind of the odd one out in that environment."

Merle's dad and Alfred's childhood friend, Sjef van Kesteren, also lived in Hyères at that point. The two would hang out together when Alfred was in Hyères, a centuries-old town of about fifty thousand residents.

"They were like the odd couple, but they had fun together," Merle remembered. Van Kesteren dressed like an English gentleman. "His shoes, pants, shirt—always in tip-top shape," she said. Alfred had just discovered sneakers, so he was walking everywhere in a pair of Nike shoes. "He persuaded my dad to also buy a pair."

Alfred had qualms about moving to France, and when prostate cancer was diagnosed, all such plans were abandoned, and he retreated back to his familiar California setting. Until the end of his life, Alfred stayed in touch with Merle, but by phone because traveling became harder. "You noticed that he became more fatigued and he had less energy to talk. But he remained interested in how things went. He wanted to know everything: Sales numbers, changes compared to the previous year, etc. He loved talking about that stuff—until the very last weeks of his life."

DEPARTURE FROM BERKELEY

Why Alfred suddenly left Berkeley in 2001 and moved to Medford, about 350 miles north of Berkeley, has always been a mystery to the people around him. He moved into a retirement home there despite the fact that "he had no family or friends there. Literally no one," his daughter Judy McCall noted.

True, his house in Berkeley was in the hills and a bit of a climb, but Alfred was still in good physical condition, so that couldn't have been a factor. Also, there were enough possibilities in down-town Berkeley to move to a more accessible house. His daughter speculated that he may have taken off the moment that he became seriously ill because he didn't want anyone to know. In Berkeley, everyone would have talked to him about it.

The way in which Alfred was dealing with his illness had already raised eyebrows with his family in the Netherlands. They sought out good doctors in the Bay Area. "But my father was rather distrustful of modern medicine and had a lot more faith in Eastern and alternative medicine," McCall said. When the illness first manifested, he tried alternative treatments, which initially worked but ultimately were insufficient. "The cancer returned dramatically."

While in Medford, Alfred made a point of visiting local roasting companies. Not everyone recognized the seventy-year-old man. "He told me he had roasted coffee his entire life and that he had a roaster in Berkeley," a coffee entrepreneur said in the local newspaper, the *Mail Tribune,* about a visit of Alfred's to his company. "He said, 'I've spent a lot of my life roasting coffee, and I had a little roaster in the Berkeley area. I said, 'You must know Alfred Peet,' and he said, 'I am Peet.'"

Alfred didn't have a good time in the apartment of the retirement home in Medford. He thought the cost of living in the home was too high and didn't like that he had to hand over the management of his finances. But the main reason he didn't like it there, according to McCall, was that he felt very constrained and missed having his privacy, as he needed to go through the general entrance and take the public elevator to reach his apartment. Soon, he moved to nearby Ashland, to live in a similar retirement home. He had an apartment on the ground floor with a front door and back door, and room for his car. It reinforced his independence, which he liked.

"Women over there fancied him," Alfred's daughter remembered and she laughed when she thought of how her father had tried to evade his admirers, indicating that the back door had come in handy.

CAPTURED ON FILM

The only existing film of Alfred (as far as I know) dates back to that period in Ashland. Two filmmakers interviewed him for their aforementioned documentary on America's coffee culture, *Coffee Culture USA.* As he walks toward the camera, the man in his late seventies begins to talk, his distinct Dutch accent hard to miss. A few sentences into the conversation, Alfred lashes out: "If I look at the bigger coffee houses, the type of drinks, they are so far away from coffee." Some coffee places, he said, look more like "glorified milkbars," referring to the latte trend (and Starbucks, possibly). "And when I looked at the sizes of such coffees . . . it hasn't got anything to do with coffee culture."

With death nearing, Alfred felt he was running out of time, and he wanted to finish one last job, which he had started years before. During a trip to the Amazon, he decided to write down everything he knew about coffee roasting. After that trip, he had about thirty pages of technical instructions. Alfred wanted to turn it into a book and asked Joan Nielsen to coauthor the book with him. They spent two days together discussing the idea, but due to various circumstances, the book never materialized.

They went to a restaurant Alfred liked, to which he insisted on driving. "I ordered iced tea, and so did he," Nielsen remembered. "But Alfred seemed disappointed, asking, 'Do you think they'll have champagne?' I took off for the kitchen and got two glasses and the champagne. He was dying, but still full of surprises, and full of life."

The next day, the ritual repeated itself. "I arrived a little late at the restaurant and he was waiting for me, with his face turned toward the sun. We ordered mussels and a bottle of Sancerre. Alfred wasn't depressed. He knew he had little time left but seemed to have accepted that."

McCall visited her father twice when he lived in Medford and Ashland. The first time was very pleasant, but the second time was awkward. "He started to lecture me about my dogs. What did my dad know about dogs? He had never had one. He had that weird way of addressing me, playing the part of the reproachful parent."

Had it been a hidden and clumsy message to tell those who stayed behind to take care of each other? We'll never know. All we know is that he died a few days after McCall visited him.

A NICE TRIBUTE

Alfred died from prostate cancer on August 29, 2007. The company announced his death the next day without mentioning the cause. In the stores, a picture of Alfred was placed on the counters, with a written tribute, and on the Peet's weblog, there was a short "In Memoriam" with pictures and a video. Soon, customers began to add their comments and personal memories of Alfred. These memories can still be read on the blog and are a touching tribute to the coffee entrepreneur.

In the responses, a large contingent proudly called itself "Peetniks," a term that was coined in the sixties to describe Peet's fans. People posted memories dating back to the early days of the store on Vine Street, when Alfred was roasting coffee, as well as memories from children who accompanied their parents. A soldier who had to go overseas at the time mentioned that he had worried that he hadn't brought enough Peet's coffee to survive.

There were also customers who had lived in the Bay Area but then moved elsewhere and were pained to leave Peet's behind. They felt happy with the web store and one of them mentioned that their UPS driver began to drink Peet's coffee. A coffee lover from Puerto Rico mourned the loss of "Don Alfred." Personal lives were forever changed by the meetings that took place at Peet's. There were even marriages that had come about between people who had been standing in line at the store.

One customer wrote, "I drank my first real coffee at Peet's in 1966." This sentiment is repeated many times over. "Love at first sip," some called it. Someone else said, "There were many followers, but Alfred couldn't be copied." Some people wrote long stories with beautiful memories of the rituals around drinking coffee, but there are also some concise and telling characterizations: "Peet was the definition of quality." One customer said, "Thank you, Mr. Peet, for making our lives so much better."

A day after the company announced Alfred's death, newspapers and press agencies in the United States published extensive articles about the "spiritual father of gourmet coffee." The *New York Times* wrote that Alfred Peet was "the leader of the coffee revolution," while the *Washington Post* said that he was "the Dutchman who started the gourmet coffee craze." To the *Los Angeles Times*, he was "the father of our coffee culture," and the *San Francisco Chronicle* remembered him as the "pioneer of specialty coffee."

Founder of famous Berkeley restaurant Chez Panisse, Alice Waters, told the *New York Times* that Alfred introduced her to quality coffee: "Everybody was drinking coffee that came out of a can. But Alfred was a purist rooted in the European tradition. He taught us a new way to look at food, wine, and coffee—paying attention to the preparation, the ritual, and understanding how the beans and ingredients were grown."

Jerry Baldwin said to the same paper that he and the founders of Starbucks had learned everything from Alfred. "He generously shared with us how to cup, to roast, and to blend, and instilled his uncompromising standards. I'll always be in his debt."

Corby Kummer, author of the book *The Joy of Coffee*, wrote an obituary in the *Los Angeles Times*, saying that, thanks to Alfred, everyone can now order coffee according to his or her own taste. "That one man's preference could shape international taste is extraordinary

. . . Anyone who considers his or her own taste in coffee to be the only right taste is making Alfred Peet, somewhere, smile."

However, in the country of his birth, the Netherlands, there was little attention paid to his death. The biggest paper in the country, *De Telegraaf*, published a short article on September 1 entitled, "Dutchman who taught the United States how to drink coffee." The national broadcasting company and news organization, NOS, featured him more broadly a few days later, with about the same headline as *De Telegraaf*. Nonetheless, Alfred's impact on the world was clear.

THE INHERITANCE

Alfred was cremated and his ashes were scattered at sea, off the California coast. When his will was revealed, it showed that he had donated almost all of his money to charities. A large part went to organizations for the elderly and handicapped, but he also donated to art institutions and a children's hospital. He did reserve some money for his two grandchildren and the children of his nephews in the Netherlands. Alfred was a wealthy man when Peet's was sold but the exact amount he received is not known, nor do we know his exact estate at the time of his death. His daughter confirmed that there weren't any millions left.

Among all the papers she received after her father's death, she found a handwritten sheet containing one of Peet's best-kept secrets: the recipe for the classic coffee blend, Major Dickason's.

On Sunday, October 14, 2007, there was a private memorial service for Alfred in the Berkeley City Club, a beautiful and historic hotel in the center of town. Family from the Netherlands had come over. His daughter, Judy McCall spoke, and so did Jerry Baldwin, Jim Reynolds, Mary Williams, Gordon Bowker, and Sal Bonavita.

Laura Glen Louis, already a writer by then, recited a poem, "An Exacting Man," which she dedicated to Alfred:

> ...
>
> *You were a hard nut, Mister Peet.*
> *But you were also sweet of heart in a hairshirt glove.*
> *I found a lump, you phoned a friend,*
> *got a surgeon, like that. Some kind of thinking of.*
> *Every other month, my fellow immigrant,*
> *You at Red Cross rolled up your sleeve*
> *and with regularity worthy of a penitent*
> *gave back blood for the countrymen of liberators*
> *at whose feet . . . thank God . . . freed*
> *from Nazi toil but not the deeds.*
> *The rest unsaid. Unpayable.*
> *Exacting man. But, you were hard taught.*
> *In youth, from you, was much exacted.*

Zev Siegl was on his way to the service, but when he arrived at Seattle International Airport to check in for his flight he learned that the airport in Oakland was closed temporarily due to a thick blanket of fog. By the time the airport reopened, the memorial service for Alfred Peet had already begun. Siegl decided to pay tribute by drinking coffee at a Peet's at the airport in Seattle. Looking back, he said, "Through coffee Alfred was able to build up beautiful relationships with other people. In that way, he created a way of life that fitted him perfectly but that also made many people happy."

PRIZE FOR ALFRED

A year after this death, Alfred received a posthumous prize from the most important coffee organization in the United States. The prize was also named after him. Undoubtedly, he would have seen the humor of it and might have quipped, "They probably didn't want me to come to fetch it in person." Perhaps there was some truth to that.

The Alfred Peet Passionate Cup Award had been started by the Specialty Coffee Association of America (SCAA). In 1992, Alfred had already received a Lifetime Achievement Award from this organization. The award goes to people who've made an extraordinary contribution to America's coffee industry. When he received the award, he was not concerned with his popularity, admonishing the audience about adding flavors to coffee. That was a lucrative business for many, but to the coffee purist and master that was a mortal sin. Some left the room, but Alfred wasn't bothered and simply continued his tirade. "Typical Peet," said others, who stayed in the room.

The Alfred Peet Passionate Cup Award is an individual award in recognition of a person "whose commitment to coffee is representative of a general passion for life and who has demonstrated a consistent record of driving progress through passion." The prize was named after Alfred because the SCAA saw Alfred as the "father of specialty coffee" and recognized his "unique focus and advocacy of what we are doing."

No doubt, Alfred would have felt honored. But he would have undoubtedly had something to say about it, too.

"Talented roastmasters will keep the company going. Day in, day out."

—Alfred Peet

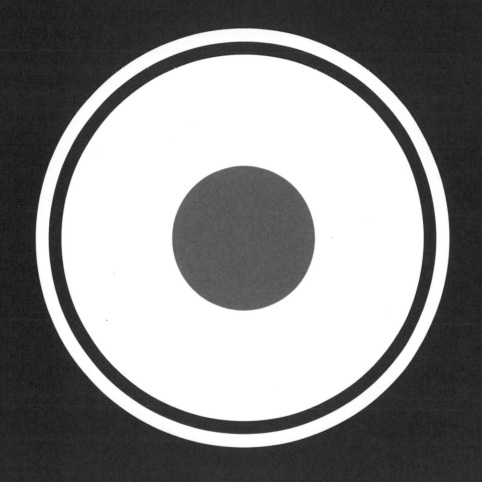

11

THE NEW PEET'S

"he company was not for sale," CEO Patrick O'Dea of Peet's wrote to his employees in July 2012, explaining how the German investor Joh. A. Benckiser (JAB) had made a bid of $1 billion, and the board of directors had already agreed to the acquisition. "JAB made an unsolicited offer to buy the company that the board of directors determined was in the best interests of shareholders to accept." The price of the stock went up quickly after that. JAB essentially offered 29 percent more than the value of the individual shares prior to the bid. "You should be immensely proud that you have built Peet's into such a valuable company by focusing on doing things the right way," O'Dea wrote.

Ever since Peet's had gone public in 2001, there had been regular rumors about the company being acquired. Starbucks was mentioned most often as a possible candidate for the acquisition. But the Dutch coffee brand Douwe Egberts also seemed interested in the Bay Area company, according to Michiel Herkemij, who used to lead Douwe Egberts. "I looked at it very seriously at the time. In the United States, but especially on the West Coast, Peet's has a very special position. For me, it was interesting to do the research and see how they had made that happen."

With a delegation of his company, Herkemij went to the West Coast to solve the riddle. "We contemplated Peet's as a candidate for our plans of mergers and acquisitions. In the end, we decided against it because there were other opportunities for Douwe Egberts, especially in Europe, but also in Asia."

The company that did make an offer, the investment company JAB, manages the capital of the German Reimann family. At the end of 2015, JAB director Peter Harf mentioned in the German magazine *Manager Magazin* that the family had €20 billion in capital. The family fortune comes from the German chemical company Benckiser, which later merged with the British company Reckitt. Examples of consumer products of the company are Calgon, Strepsils, and Durex.

In the past, JAB liked to operate on the sidelines, but when they acquired Peet's and the big deals that followed, it became harder to stay hidden. The company's leadership team consists of Bart Becht (Dutch), Olivier Goudet (French), and the aforementioned Harf (German).

Becht became famous for being one of the executives of Reckitt Benckiser, which he expanded in an impressive way. His income grew with it, and frequently—Becht has been called "the best paid executive of Great Britain," which would inevitably lead to a fierce discussion about his income (£90 million in 2009). He also topped another list—that of generous philanthropists. In 2010, he put £110 million into his Bart Becht Foundation, which supports Save the Children and Doctors without Borders, among other charity organizations.

In 2010, JAB bought a great number of companies, first within the market of luxury products (the cosmetics company Coty and the fashion brand Jimmy Choo), after which JAB focused on the coffee market. First, there was the acquisition of Peet's (197 shops), then Caribou (610 shops), followed by the Swedish coffee chain

Espresso House (200 shops) and the Danish firm Baresso (47 shops). In 2013, Peet's and Douwe Egberts ended up with the same owner, when JAB also acquired the Dutch coffee company for about €7.5 billion. In line with the beliefs of Luxemburg-based JAB, the different companies continued operating independently.

Soon after JAB started acquiring coffee companies, analyses were published about the underlying motives for the initiative. Some people argued it would develop into an attack on Starbucks, a fight among giants, with Starbucks on the one hand and the combined Peet's, Caribou, Douwe Egberts, and Espresso House on the other, but that theory was soon debunked.

The identities of the companies JAB bought were too different, and they couldn't be turned into one brand. Furthermore, there is a difference between chains that only sell coffee via stores, and companies like Peet's, that also have a strong position on the shelves of supermarkets. And there was a difference in company structure— some of JAB's chains work with franchises, but that's not the case with Peet's, which manages all its own stores (as does Starbucks).

BRAND BUILDERS

After Peet's was acquired, Baldwin planned on retiring, but JAB requested that he, along with a few other board members, stay on. He described JAB as a "brand builder" and said that the investor was "heavily engaged in wanting to build up the brand further." Additionally, Baldwin remembered how Becht, along with other executives from JAB, came to Peet's for a barista training. "After they had examined our expectations for the market of single-serve K-cups, we were told to buy another machine to make more K-cups. That wasn't a small investment, but millions of dollars."

According to some sources, more funding became available by stretching the payment terms of Peet's, which for many vendors came as a shock. Under the new owners, Peet's would stretch the payment terms to sixty days, which is not unusual for bigger companies. By paying bills after sixty days, Peet's suddenly had more cash flow.

JAB's next step within the coffee market seemed to shed light on what their plans had been all along. In 2014, the investor added Douwe Egberts to the coffee branch of the American company Mondelez, and owner of the brands Jacobs and Carte Noire. Thus "the largest coffee company in the world" came into being, according to JAB and Mondelez. JAB got 51 percent and Mondelez 49 percent of the newly formed Jacobs Douwe Egberts, which is headquartered in the Netherlands.

It also became clear that JAB didn't perceive Jacobs Douwe Egberts as a chain of coffee stores, even though Douwe Egberts had its own stores and, years prior, had become the owner of the Dutch coffee chain Coffee Company. With Jacobs Douwe Egberts, the emphasis is on the sale of beans, ground coffee, and coffee cups for homes, offices, hotels, and restaurants.

The claim of "the largest coffee company in the world" is not quite accurate, but the message of the enterprise that gave itself that title became apparent. The Swiss company Nestlé (owner of such brands as Nespresso and Dolce Gusto) is seen as a market leader in the coffee world in revenue, but the company also focuses on other products, which makes Jacobs Douwe Egberts the industry leader.

The analysis that JAB has had its eye on market leader Nestlé was validated when they acquired Green Mountain Coffee Roasters in 2015 for $13 billion. In the last few years, the company gained a strong position in single-serve cups (K-cups) and, as such, is a competitor of Nestlé.

But what would happen next, once JAB's coffee empire surpassed Nestlé? There are two main theories that are diametrically opposed. On the one hand, people say that Becht, Goudet, and Harf are brand builders. At the acquisition of Peet's, Becht referred to "an investment in a first-class brand." They lead their companies in a very disciplined way, but are not primarily concerned with cost. As Baldwin already noted, they are not afraid to make large investments.

But there are other people and "JAB watchers" who think there might be a completely different scenario at play. They see financial engineering on a large scale. In total, JAB has already invested almost $30 billion in the acquisition of coffee companies. With such acquisitions, the investor has rearranged the coffee market and has made its own interests in it more valuable, after which it might seek a way out. The latter would happen via the stock market, and with a large return on investment, or so some analysts think.

Slowly, the plans for Peet's within that much larger company also became more apparent. A new CEO at the helm made sure the company received more attention in the media, proudly pointing to the important and decades long tradition of Peet's in the American coffee world. And Peet's itself became a company acquiring others.

TOO MODEST

"It struck me that Peet's is rather modest. We don't beat the drum too often," CEO Dave Burwick said during a conversation in 2015. "I think this may have come from Alfred Peet. The company

assimilated that behavior and Jerry Baldwin continued it." To
the surprise of Burwick, who became the CEO in 2012 shortly
after the acquisition, the logo wasn't even printed on the take-out
cups anymore. "In 2015, you can't do that sort of thing anymore.
There's a lot of competition from other brands and, because of
that, you really have to tell your story."

Burwick used to be the CEO of Weight Watchers in North
America, but it seems they recruited him for Peet's because he had
had twenty years of experience with PepsiCo before that, where he
held several leadership roles in brand and general management.
Burwick also sits on the board of directors of Boston Beer
Company, and therefore has insight into the craft beer industry,
which has many parallels to the coffee business.

While Burwick never met Alfred Peet in person, he experienced
Peet's for the first time when he came to the Bay Area. "It's typical
for the region," he said. "But I've always seen Jerry as an extension
of Alfred Peet. He's erudite and really cares about coffee. Jerry
passed on these values to the next generation within the company."

Another connection with Alfred Peet is Jim Reynolds, who
has retired but still visits the company on a weekly basis. "It's very
special that we've been around for fifty years and that the family of
roastmasters consists of only three people: Peet, Reynolds, and now
Doug Welsh."

Burwick explained that the search for better coffee is still prev-
alent. "In that respect, nothing has changed since the beginning
of the company. The mission is the same; we just use other words
to describe it. When you, like Peet's, have an authentic story and
such a clear mission, then customers don't only buy your product,
but also buy the accompanying story. You can compare it to Apple,

a company that democratized creativity with the slogan 'Think different.'"

Burwick talked about the company stock and his vision, but as soon as he heard the observations of an outsider, he fell silent to take it all in. He then explained that Peet's was a good example of a company that would be better off as a private rather than public company. "You can see that from the way in which the company used the stores. More was earned from the expansion into supermarkets and because of that, the development of the stores was put on hold."

But people won't buy Peet's if they don't know the experience with the coffee stores, Burwick concluded, and under his leadership, Peet's started investing more into its stores to "make the brand stronger."

Profitability and revenue have risen sharply in the last few years. In 2011, the year of the acquisition by JAB, revenue numbers were $371 million. These increased to $800 million in 2016.

But Burwick is even more ambitious. He wants Peet's "to become the most appreciated premium coffee brand," and the company has to lead in employee engagement. Burwick envisions a growth of five hundred stores and, around 2019, he hopes to hit a revenue number of $1 billion. Owner JAB even thinks there's more potential than that. "They see Peet's as a crown jewel, a super-premium brand and a company that can have revenue numbers between $3 to $4 billion."

Burwick thinks that the strongest growth lies in sales to supermarkets—one in every twenty-five households buys Peet's in the supermarket. There's a lot of potential there. The phenomenon of single cups is growing strongly for Peet's, to the tune of 50 percent per year. "The trend is that people want things to be easier. It won't take much longer before that segment of the market will outrun the premium coffees on the shelf and the market for budget coffee."

But revenue in the stores has increased as well. "In the United States, people are looking for an alternative to Starbucks. They have done a really great job, but it has become so ubiquitous that it has lost its specialness, so we are capitalizing on that." Both companies became famous with their dark roasts, but according to Burwick, Peet's is "bolder and smoother" than its competitor. Burwick claims that in tests between Starbucks and Peet's, customers preferred Peet's. Those results were echoed in a Peet's ad campaign from 2016 with the slogan: "Berkeley, home of the Seattle coffee scene."

Under Burwick, Peet's also plans to expand to China, where it works with a local partner. Additionally, in the second half of 2015, the company made an important move by acquiring two prominent coffee companies from the so-called "third wave": Stumptown Coffee Roasters from Portland and Intelligentsia from Chicago.

THIRD WAVE

No one knows when or who started the so-called "third wave," but starting in the nineties, people began to produce lighter roasts in the United States. One can't say it was a new thing, as the lighter roasts (of quality beans) were already well known in Europe, and especially in Scandinavia. It was called "third wave" to make a distinction from "second wave" coffee companies, like Peet's, which had put specialty coffee on the map. The "first wave" refers to when coffee became widely available, although the coffee hadn't been great in terms of quality.

Filtered coffee (made per individual cup) became popular again with these third wavers. Freshness of the beans had already been important with companies like Peet's and Starbucks, but for the new coffee entrepreneurs, it became an obsession. And there was a stronger preference for so-called "single-origin coffees," which means that the harvest originates from a single plantation rather than from several plantations in the same area.

Coffee stores became hip and cool, and tattoos were almost compulsory for handling the roaster or espresso machine. Coffee roasters were also placed more prominently in the store again to draw attention to the craftsmanship quality, just like Alfred had done in his shop on Vine Street. To reinforce this image, it was even better to have a store in an industrial-type building, in a remote area.

But the most important thing was the direct relationship these new entrepreneurs tried to foster with the farmers who grew the coffee. Employees of companies such as Stumptown, Counter Culture, and Intelligentsia often visit coffee plantations in Africa, Asia, and Central and South America. They try to circumvent vendors and do direct business with the coffee farmers, so that they can pay the farmers better and help them at the same time with the improvement of overall quality.

These new kids on the block were quickly visited by members of the second wave who wanted to see for themselves what all the hullabaloo about the "new coffee revolution" was about. Naturally, there was plenty of criticism: "They have no idea what they're doing" and "It's all about marketing and nothing but marketing" were some of the complaints made. But there was one thing everyone agreed upon—the third-wavers were very motivated to make good coffee. The coffee flavor doesn't always meet the expectations of the second-wavers, but it's made with a passion that they recognize in themselves and in Alfred Peet.

Alfred managed to experience the third wave, but he didn't think much of single-origin coffee or the embellished descriptions for coffee (a tendency we are familiar with in the world of wine). That said, he must have liked the fact that coffee roasters and roastmasters were seen in the stores again, and he must also have appreciated the passion with which they did their work.

SCALING THEIR SMALLNESS

Peet's bought Stumptown in October 2015 because of their strong position in the market for cold brew. It's the latest coffee trend, even though the process to make coffee with cold water is an old concept. Making coffee with cold water results in a milder coffee with less acidity. You can't compare it to iced coffee, which is made by mixing hot coffee with ice cubes.

Less than a month after the Stumptown acquisition, Peet's became the largest shareholder in Intelligentsia. Just like Duane Sorenson of Stumptown, cofounder Doug Zell of Intelligentsia started his coffee career at Peet's. He referred to that at the time of the sale and said he was glad to be working at Peet's again. Just like Stumptown, Intelligentsia is known for its direct trade with coffee farmers, but it's also famous for its high-quality espresso. The current espresso culture, in which baristas have become demigods, was in large part started by Intelligentsia.

The acquisitions happened because of the "exploding American market for super premium coffees and the rise of a new generation of coffee drinkers," CEO Dave Burwick declared in a conversation about the acquisition. The eighteen- to thirty-four-year-old age group has enough money to spend on coffee but also buy premium brands of other drinks, such as specialty beers and juices. "To pull in a larger part of that market, it's important that Peet's has a varied and appealing menu of coffee brands. We're seeing a whole new generation of customers. They are people who want variation and new experiences. My oldest daughter is in her twenties and she goes to three different coffee stores. One is close to her work, but the other two she visits because she wants to experiment with new flavors or wants to see new ways of making coffee. There's not one single coffee store that can offer all that."

Stumptown and Intelligentsia operate under Peet's, but they are managed as separate companies. That approach is in alignment with the ideas of the owner of JAB, according to Burwick. "When an acquired company becomes just a brand in your portfolio, you will take the soul out of the company and it will cease to exist."

Through the distribution network of Peet's, however, the coffees of Stumptown and Intelligentsia have become available to a wider audience. The six hundred trucks of Peet's will now also pick up these coffees to distribute to supermarkets. There are high expectations for the sale of cold coffee through supermarkets. Using the distribution network of Peet's means that Stumptown doesn't have to go after the market itself. "We basically scale their smallness," Burwick explains. He won't be leading the next moves for Peet's, however, as in February 2018, Burwick decided to accept the offer to become CEO of the Boston Beer Company, where he was already on the board of directors since 2005.

NEW STORE DESIGN

Jerry Baldwin was leading the way. Over there, on the other side of the street, we saw the Peet's store. "It's very different from what you've seen thus far," Baldwin explained. He managed the company longer than Alfred, and he opened the door to the newly designed store on Chestnut Street in San Francisco. It's a so-called pilot store, but since then, dozens of stores have been transformed in a similar way.

Details from the first Peet's, such as the wood decor and the typography of the menu, are still recognizable in the interior. The logo retains its Indonesian motif, but the back wall, which is covered with plants, the light, the art on the walls, and the hip baristas are more in keeping with the trendy coffee stores one can find elsewhere in the city.

Still there's an important difference here, and that's the spirit of Alfred Peet: The coffee beans themselves. They are prominently sold in the front part of the shop. There's also an employee who explains Mocha, Yirgacheffe, Antigua, and Major Dickason's coffees and how to prepare them. A tradition of fifty years is still alive and well.

"Alfred Peet was the father of our coffee culture."

—*Los Angeles Times*, August 2007

AFTERWORD

A LAZY SUNDAY MORNING

I f you look closely, you can see Alkmaar, the city where Alfred was born. How many customers will have seen the picture on the wall of the first Peet's store in Berkeley? How many will have wondered why there's a picture of a walled, European city? The image conjures up a different time, one that goes back to the seventeenth century, when a captain working for the powerful Dutch East India Company may have been the first Dutchman to discover coffee in Yemen. The history of coffee took a crucial turn. No other Dutchman in the coffee world after that had as large an impact until Alfred Peet started his coffee store in Berkeley.

A short distance away from this picture, one can see the original storage bins for coffee, made by the Chinese carpenters from Oakland, who, following Alfred's instructions, built them more than fifty years ago. From the ceiling, the remarkable lamps can still be admired, which, with their red light, some have described as creating an atmosphere of a fourteenth-century lab. You can smell the obvious and heavy scent of coffee that, for fifty years, has lingered in the store.

After ordering a cup of the famous Major Dickason's, made to honor Alfred, I walk back to the entryway to enjoy a lazy Sunday morning on a bench by the window at Peet's. To the right of me, I see the sixties logo of Peet's Coffee, Tea & Spices in gold letters.

It's busy. In front of me, two friends are busy talking about— who knows? The week that's behind them? A man is doing a crossword, and a student divides his attention between papers in his left hand and his laptop on the right. Another man enters, not for the first time—it's as if he's coming home.

"Good morning. How can I help you?" One of the employees asks him. It's not hard to imagine hearing this from Alfred, with his heavy Dutch accent. In fact, after all the stories, it's not hard to imagine what Peet's looked like back in 1966. Suddenly, I see the provocative "John Paul" entering the store, ready to be chased away by Alfred. And there are the curious faces of new customers, who come in—no—are drawn in by the scent of freshly roasted coffee. They try a cup of the dark roast and are shocked. There's so much flavor there—one needs to recover from that. I see Alfred walking to his roaster, in his signature outfit—pants, shirt, tie, and shopcoat. People follow him with their gaze: What special coffee will he conjure up now? Behind me, I hear the chatter of people who finish their coffees in the street. Coffee entrepreneurs drop in and are impressed, hoping to unravel Mr. Peet's secret. This is the legacy of the godfather of specialty coffee.

At that bench by the entryway, I reflect on Alfred's statement, "Coffee tells my story." I take another sip of the Major Dickason's and savor it. In it, you have everything that you need at such a moment. But when I take the next sip, I think back to all the stories I've heard about Alfred. After yet another sip, the faces appear of all those who played a role in all these stories and who, thanks to Alfred and his coffee, developed their own. But it's also the story of all the people around me, the ones who don't just come here for their daily coffee fix but for whom Peet's has become an important part of their lives. That impact—that is probably the most important story of Alfred's coffee.

APPENDIX

ACKNOWLEDGMENTS

B ut how did you end up with Alfred Peet?" has been a question that was asked repeatedly during the writing of this book. This question recurred especially in the Netherlands, where Alfred is barely known. It all started with Mark Pendergrast's book *Uncommon Grounds*, which is a remarkable history of the American coffee industry. Later, the author told me in a Skype chat about his meeting with Alfred Peet. He said that Alfred didn't like that he had dedicated his book to him. The dedication was indeed odd, since Pendergrast only spent two pages on Alfred in a book that has more than three hundred and fifty pages. But it did indicate the enormous influence Alfred had on the American coffee world. I want to thank Pendergrast for leading me to Alfred Peet.

I conducted more than forty interviews for this book, and they were conversations I'll remember for a long time. The coffee business is about people, as I was told time and again. I hope this is also one of the impressions readers have of this book.

I'm particularly indebted to one interviewee, and that is one of the cofounders of Starbucks, Jerry Baldwin. Without his cooperation, which he promised in 2013, this book would not have been possible. Baldwin opened doors for me to other entrepreneurs and friends of Alfred's.

Finding Alfred's relatives was not easy. After searching several archives, there was but one option left: An address somewhere in the Netherlands. Alfred's older sister no longer lived there, but fortunately, my letter was forwarded by the new residents and, in the beginning of 2014, I received a sudden phone call from Rudolf van der Flier, Alfred's nephew. Without his interest in the idea about his influential uncle and the promise of his then ninety-seven-year-old mother Gertrude van der Flier-Peet to talk about her brother, I couldn't have fleshed-out the family history. They connected me with other relatives and fortunately, everyone was happy to share stories.

The author Adah Bakalinsky was extremely important for this book. I never interviewed her or talked to her, but thanks to Roast-master Emeritus Jim Reynolds, I received two recordings of long conversations that she had with Alfred in August 1980 and June 1982. She and her husband were friends of Alfred's. When the USB stick arrived in the mail, it was as if a lump of gold had just been delivered. To hear Alfred talk was a great insight, but also, with everything he said, the story gained an important extra layer. The conversations were candid and at times painful. I'm grateful that Bakalinsky gave her permission to use the audio recordings.

The people at Peet's helped me find pictures for this book and CEO David Burwick spoke to me twice with valuable insights into the trajectory of the company. Their enthusiasm for this book was very special to me.

I want to thank my wife, Nuria, for her constant interest in this book. My son and daughter often joined me on Saturdays to get beans from the different coffee stores in the neighborhood. They came with all sorts of questions, such as "Is there a coffee for children?" which reminded me of the question I had heard in Honduras, "How do you like the coffee?"—the question that started this book. I dedicate this book to my father, Jaap, who once owned a building company, then became an independent contractor, and was the first entrepreneur I got to know.

—JASPER HOUTMAN

SOURCES

This book was based on interviews, research in archives, and secondary literature about coffee and publications in the media. In this book, Alfred Peet tells his story in his own words thanks to two conversations that he had with the American author Adah Bakalinsky in 1980 and 1982. He consented to interviews very infrequently, but the few he did give with the newspapers the *East Bay Express,* the *Mail Tribune, NRC Handelsblad,* and *Inc* were very worthwhile. I also used statements Alfred Peet made in the documentary *Coffee Culture USA*, which are, presumably, the only film images that were made of him.

INTERVIEWS

Alfred Peet, recorded interviews by Adah Bakalinsky, August 1980 and June 1982.

Bonnie Grossman, friend of Alfred Peet's in Berkeley, in discussion with the author.

Chris Jordan, director of quality at Starbucks Coffee Trading, former CEO Verve Coffee Roasters, Coffee Manufactory, in discussion with the author.

Dave Burwick, CEO Peet's Coffee & Tea, in discussion with the author.

Dick de Kock, cofounder Coffee Company, now coffee advisor, in discussion with the author.

Gertrude van der Flier-Peet, Alfred Peet's eldest sister, in discussion with the author.

Gordon Bowker, cofounder Starbucks, Red Hook Ale Brewery, in discussion with the author.

Hans-Dieter Mallasch, cofounder German coffee firm List & Beisler, supplier of Peet's, in discussion with the author.

Joe Paff, pupil of Alfred Peet and owner of coffee firm Gold Rush Coffee, Eureka, CA, recorded interview by Willem Boot.

Jerry Baldwin, cofounder Starbucks, chairman Peet's Coffee & Tea, winefarmer in Sonoma Valley, in discussion with the author.

Jim Reynolds, roastmaster emeritus Peet's Coffee & Tea, in discussion with the author.

Joan Nielsen, coauthor *The Great Coffee Book*, in discussion with the author.

John Weaver, former roastmaster at Peet's Coffee & Tea, founder Weaver's Coffee & Tea, in discussion with the author.

Joop Sik, member, historic society in Alkmaar (Historische Vereniging Alkmaar), in discussion with the author.

Judy McCall, Peet's daughter, in discussion with the author.

Kees van der Westen, Dutch maker of espresso machines, founder Kees van der Westen Espressionistic Works.

Laura Louis, former employee Peet's Coffee & Tea, poet, in discussion with the author.

Leigh McDonald, pupil of Alfred Peet, founder Coffee Connection in the Netherlands, partner Munduk Coffee, in discussion with the author.

Mariette Merle, niece of Alfred Peet, who, with her husband, Bruno Merle, owns a vineyard in France, in discussion with the author.

Marc Chavannes, former correspondent *NRC Handelsblad* in the Unites States, in discussion with the author.

Mark Pendergrast, author of *Uncommon Grounds*, in discussion with the author.

Mary Williams, senior vice president of Coffee for Starbucks, now retired; in discussion with the author.

Michiel Herkemij, former CEO Douwe Egberts, in discussion with the author.

Menno Simons, Dutch coffee entrepreneur, founder Trabocca and Bocca Coffee Roasters.

Paul van Kesteren, the brother of Sjef van Kesteren, who was a close friend and brother in law of Alfred Peet.

Roel Vaessen, European Coffee Federation (ecf), in discussion with the author.

Rose van Asten and Liesbeth Sleijster, Dutch barista champions, in discussion with the author.

Ross Blum, former employee Peet's Coffee & Tea, in discussion with the author.

Rudolf van der Flier, Peet's nephew, and his sister-in-law Janneke, in discussion with the author.

Sal Bonavita, owner Peet's Coffee & Tea 1979–1984, in discussion with the author.

Shirin Moayyad, buyer at Peet's and now trainer/coffee-expert at Nespresso, in discussion with the author.

Walt Neal, former employee Peet's Coffee & Tea, in discussion with the author.

Willem Boot, Dutch coffee entrepreneur in San Francisco (Boot Coffee), owner coffee farm in Panama, in discussion with the author.

Wolfgang Dehner, cofounder German coffee firm List & Beisler, supplier of Peet's, in discussion with the author.

Zev Siegl, cofounder Starbucks, consultant/coach, in discussion with the author.

BOOKS, PERIODICALS, BLOGS & DOCUMENTARIES

"A Judge of the People." *San Francisco Chronicle*, February 7,1999.

Abecassis, Andrée. *Peet's Coffee & Tea: A History in Honor of its Twenty-Fifth Birthday.* Peet's Coffee & Tea, 1992.

"Alfred H. Peet, 1920–2007." *Peet's Coffee & Tea Blog*, http://peets.typepad.com/blog/2007/08/alfred-h-peet-2.html.

Allen, Stewart Lee. *The Devil's Cup.* New York: Ballantine Books, 2003.

Andrejczak, Matt. "Peet's CEO: We Weren't Shopping Ourselves." *MarketWatch*, July 24, 2012.

Arlington, David. "The Stimulating world of Mr Peet." *East Bay Express*, July 13, 1984.

Brouwer, C.G. *De voc in Jemen, 1614–1655.* Netherlands: J B Wolters, 1988.

Burhardt, Majka. *Coffee Story: Ethiopia.* Boston: Ninetyplus Press, 2011.

Castle, Timothy J., and Joan Nielsen. *The Great Coffee Book.* Emeryville: Ten Speed Press, 1999.

Chavannes, Marc. "McDonald's van de koffie opent elke dag een winkel." *NRC Handelsblad*, July 21, 2000.

Clark, Taylor. *Starbucked.* London: Sceptre, 2007.

Coffee Culture USA. Directors Julie van Schooten and Kenneth van Schooten, ETiT Productions, 2008, documentary.

Coolhaas, W. *Pieter van den Broecke in Azië.* Boston: Martinus Nihoff Publishers, 1962.

Cole, Tom. *A Short History of San Francisco.* Berkeley: Heyday, 2014.

de Graaff , H.J. "Herinneringen aan Alkmaar omstreeks 1900." *Alkmaars Jaarboekje*, 1965.

Evanovsky, Dennis, and Eric J. Kos. *Lost San Francisco.* London: Pavilion 2011.

Freedberg, Louis. "Peet, Berkeley Store Paved Starbucks' Way," *San Francisco Chronicle*, August 5, 2001.

Freeman, James, Caitlin Freeman, and Tara Duggan. *The Blue Bottle Craft of Coffee.* Emeryville: Ten Speed Press, 2012.

Frölke, Viktor. "Starbucks maakt van koffie een marketingconcept." *NRC Handelsblad,* January 12, 2006.

George Howell, interview Coffeegeek.com, "Berkeley, 1966," September, 2005, http://bit.ly/2pofJev.

"H. Keijzer's Coffee & Tea Shop Celebrates 150 years," *Tea & Coffee Trade Journal,* October 1, 1989.

Hammelburg, Olaf. *El camino del café/De weg van de koffie.* Rotterdam, Netherlands: Olaf Hammelburg, 2005.

James Hoffmann, *The World Atlas of Coffee, From Beans to Brewing* (Richmond Hill, Ontario: Firefly Books 2014).

Katrien Pauwels and others. *Puur koffie.* Lannoo, 2014.

Kawa, koffie ontsluierd: van koffiestruik tot kopje koffie. Nationale Plantentuin van België, 1995.

Kerouac, Jack. *On the Road.* London: Penguin Books, 1990.

Krugman, Paul. "Reagan Did It." *New York Times,* May 31, 2009.

———. "Disaster and Denial." *New York Times,* December 13, 2009.

Kummer, Corby. *The Joy of Coffee.* Boston: Houghton Mifflin Company, 2003.

———. "The Father of Our Coffee Culture." *Los Angeles Times,* September 17, 2007.

Louis, Laura Glen. *Some, Like Elephants.* Berkeley: El Léon Literary Arts, 2010.

Lucassen, Leo and Jan Lucassen. *Winnaars en verliezers.* Amsterdam: Prometheus, 2011.

Luttinger, Nina and Gregory Dicum. *The Coffee Book: Anatomy of an Industry from Crop to the Last Drop.* New York: The New Press, 2006.

Marshall, Carolyn. "Alfred H. Peet, 87, Dies; Leader of a Coffee Revolution," *New York Times,* September 3, 2007.

Maxwell, Jill Hecht. "Alfred Peet: My Biggest Mistake." *Inc,* June 1, 2001.

"Nederlander leerde Amerika koffie drinken." *NOS,* September 4, 2007, http://archive.li/eWVtk.

Noord Hollands Dagblad, March 15, 1962.

Ons blad: katholiek nieuwsblad voor Noord-Hollands, December 29, 1909.

"Peet's: Not Your Average Joe." *Bloomberg,* May 2, 2001.

Pendergrast, Mark. *Uncommon Grounds: The History of Coffee and How It Transformed Our World.* Knutsford, UK: Texere Publishing, 2001.

Raines, George. "Coffee Pioneer Alfred Peet Dies." *San Francisco Chronicle*, August 31, 2007.

Reinders, Pim, and Thera Wijsenbeek en anderen. *Koffie in Nederland*. Zutphen, Netherlands: Walburg Pers, 1994.

Robinson, Kenneth J. *"Savings and Loan Crisis." Federal Reserve History*, November 22, 2013.

Rosenfeld, Seth. *Subversives: The FBI's War on Student Radicals, and Reagan's Rise to Power.* New York: Picador, 2013

Schultz, Howard, and Dori Jones Yang. *Pour Your Heart into It: How Starbucks Built a Company One Cup at a Time.* New York: Hyperion Books, 1997.

Schwarzer, Ursula. Vermögen der Reimann-Familie beträgt rund 20 Milliarden Dollar," *Manager Magazin*, October 6, 2015.

Simmons John. *The Starbucks Story.* London: Cyan Books, 2005.

Stiles, Greg. "Peet Now Calls Medford His Home." *Mail Tribune*, June 1, 2003.

Sullivan, Patricia. "Alfred Peet; Put Buzz in Gourmet Coffee." *Washington Post*, September 1, 2007.

Tea publication from Division of Commerce Batavia (Java) Universiteitsbibliotheek Leiden, 1933.

Ukers, William H. *All About Coffee.* New York: Adams Media, 2012. University of California–Berkeley website

van Lakerveld, Peter. "Indië verloren, de rampspoed bleef uit," *Trouw*, August 12, 1995.

Various authors. *Geschiedenis van Alkmaar.* Zwolle, Netherlands: Uitgeverij Waanders, 2007.

Weissman, Michaele. *God in a Cup.* Hoboken, NJ: John Wiley & Sons, 2008.

Wennekes, Wim. *Gouden handel.* Amsterdam-Antwerpen: Atlas, 1996.

Wild, Antony. *Coffee: A Dark History.* New York: W.W. Norton & Company, 2005.

Woo, Elaine, "Herbert Hyman dies at 82; founder of Coffee Bean & Tea Leaf chain," *LA Times*. May 3, 2014.

Zara, Muhammad Yuanda. "Indonesia's Propoganda and the Independence War, 1945–1949." Nederlands Instituut voor Oorlogsdocumentatie; https://www.niod.nl/en/projects/indonesia%E2%80%99s-propaganda-and-indepen-dence-war-1945-1949

Not to underestimate a source: All the coffee companies here and abroad, where, in addition to enjoying great coffee, I always learned something new.

See also: www.alfredpeetbook.com

INDEX

First published in the United States in 2018 by Roundtree Press
Originally published by Business Contact in 2016
Text copyright © 2016 Jasper Houtman

Translated by Inez Hollander Lake

Photo Credits: 1, 10 © Peet family; 2 © Ancestry.com; 3, 4 © Regionaal Archief Alkmaar
(Archives Alkmaar); 5 © U.S. Naturalization Record Index; 6 © Berkeleyplaques.org; 7, 9,
11, 12, 13, 14, 21, 25 © Peet's Coffee; 8 © Frank Denman; 15 © David Lance Goines; 16,
17, 18, 19, 20, 22, 24 © Jasper Houtman; 23 © Stuart Lirette

Fragment of the poem "An Exacting Man" by Laura Glen Louis is used by permission.
From *Some, Like Elephants*, El Léon Literary Arts, 2010

Publisher: CHRIS GRUENER
Creative Director: IAIN MORRIS
Managing Editor: JAN HUGHES
Editorial Assistant: MASON HARPER
Designer: ROB DOLGAARD
Proofreader: LUCY WALKER

Library of Congress Cataloging-in-Publication Data available.

ISBN: 978-1-944903-38-1

Design by ROB DOLGAARD
Cover design by IAIN MORRIS

10 9 8 7 6 5 4 3 2 1

Manufactured in China

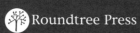

Roundtree Press
149 Kentucky Street, Suite 7
Petaluma, CA 94952
www.roundtreepress.com